CHALMERIANA:

OR

A COLLECTION OF PAPERS,
LITERARY AND POLITICAL

BY

George Hardinge

TOGETHER WITH

Mr. Ireland's
Vindication of his Conduct

RESPECTING THE PUBLICATION
OF THE
SUPPOSED SHAKESPEARE MSS.

Being a Preface or Introduction to
A Reply to the Critical Labors of Mr. Malone in his
"ENQUIRY INTO THE AUTHENTICITY OF
CERTAIN PAPERS"

BY

George Steevens

AUGUSTUS M. KELLEY · PUBLISHERS
NEW YORK 1971

Published by
FRANK CASS AND COMPANY LIMITED
67 Great Russell Street, London WC1B 3BT

Published in the United States by
Augustus M. Kelley, Publishers
New York, New York 10010

New preface Copyright © 1971 Arthur Freeman

Chalmeriana

| First edition | 1800 |
| Reprint of First edition with a new preface | 1971 |

Mr. Ireland's Vindication

| First edition | 1796 |
| Reprint of First edition with a new preface | 1971 |

ISBN 0 678 05137 2

Library of Congress Catalog Card No. 76-96370

Printed in Great Britain

EIGHTEENTH CENTURY SHAKESPEARE
No. 23

General Editor : Professor Arthur Freeman, Boston University

CHALMERIANA

Together with

Mr. Ireland's
Vindication of his Conduct

A complete list of titles in this series
is included at the end of this volume.

PREFACE

Chalmeriana

We present George Hardinge's pseudonymous *Chalmeriana* primarily as an example of the sort of amateur flyting which occupied time and reciprocal energy throughout the eighteenth century on matters Shakespearean. Whatever small literary merit the satire may possess, its primary function and claim to memory is as part of a complicated dispute about editorial method and historical truth. Neither object sustains *Chalmeriana*, but among such squibs the present is by no means the least compelling. Wit and disinterested antagonism are on Hardinge's side, and one need not be embarrassed to read the counterblast to Chalmers which Malone, as King Log, chose not to concoct.

George Hardinge (1743–1816), Byron's 'waggish Welsh judge' [*Don Juan*, xiii, 88], comes down to us as an amiable, jocular, irreverent commentator on the inflated editorial 'problems' of the day. The butts of his earlier Shakespearean satire included Malone (at least twice) and Ritson; no partiality is shown in his cheerful administration of the lash to clumsy reasoning and special pleading of a sort which could never satisfy a cautious legalist, in the Ireland matter. *Chalmeriana* is hardly a masterpiece of scholarship or review, but its irony exemplifies a whole population's response to questions puffed far beyond the factual limits they required, and seldom if ever drawing attention to the more general ambiguities of method and intent they evoked. Curiously, it is

PREFACE

the most methodological commentator, George Chalmers, whom Hardinge here chooses to bait, but the force of the satire might as well have been directed against any number of lesser apologists. Our reprint is prepared from a copy of the first, and only separate edition, in the Birmingham Public Library, collating a^{4}B–F^{8}G^7[G8 blank?], with no cancels. Hardinge's *Miscellaneous Works* were edited after his death by his friend the anecdotalist George Nichols (1818, 3 v.), and include this unrevised text. I have compared the present copy with two others, in the British Museum and at Harvard.

December, 1970   A. F.

PREFACE

A Vindication

George Steevens is apparently responsible for the traditional attribution of *A Vindication* to Thomas Caldecott (1744-1833), bibliophile and Shakespearean, the 'Temple Friend' of Ireland, but on no given grounds. In the absence of other evidence there seems no reason to suspect anyone but Samuel himself, who gives, as always, his Norfolk Street address in lieu of signing his preface and text, and speaks throughout in the first person and of 'my son', William Henry. Perhaps Steevens was only casting characteristic aspersions on the ability of Samuel to compose even his own defence. We have retained the dubious ascription only to minimize confusion in cataloguing.

A Vindication explains itself quite simply. Engaged in a full-length 'refutation' of Malone's devastating *Inquiry*, which had exposed in April W. H. Ireland's fraudulent 'Shakespearean' papers as the clumsiest of fabrications, Samuel was confronted in December by the completely embarassing printed confession of his own son (*An Authentic Account, &c.*, no. 21 in our series). Desiring to reply at once, Samuel apparently pared off the following pages and rushed out an answer. He details his motives in the Advertisement, pp. iii–iv, below.

The fuller assault, less some repetitions from this prior pamphlet, appeared as *An Investigation of Mr. Malone's Claim to the Character of a Scholar* (our no. 24, also dated 1796). If the latter date is

PREFACE

not fictitious, December was a busy month for the Irelands. Our reprint is prepared from a copy of the original edition in the Birmingham Public Library, compared with copies in the British Museum and two (including the Tite) at Harvard. It collates [ ]^{2}A–F^4, with no cancels.

December, 1970   A. F.

CHALMERIANA:

OR

A COLLECTION OF PAPERS

LITERARY AND POLITICAL,

ENTITLED,

LETTERS, VERSES, &c. OCCASIONED BY READING A LATE HEAVY SUPPLEMENTAL APOLOGY FOR THE BELIEVERS IN THE SHAKESPEARE PAPERS BY GEORGE CHALMERS, F. R. S. S. A.

ARRANGED AND PUBLISHED

By Mr. OWEN JUNIOR, of Paper Buildings, Inner Temple;

ASSISTED BY HIS FRIEND AND CLERK,

Mr. JASPER HARGRAVE.

REPRINTED FROM THE MORNING CHRONICLE, IN WHICH THEY FIRST APPEARED.

Allez jufqu' ou l'Aurore en naiffant voit l' Hydafpe,
Cherchez pour l'y graver le plus precieux JASPE:
Sur mon tombeau futur courez pour l' énoncer,
Et en lettres *de plomb* allez ces vers placer;
" De fa plume épuifant la péfante énergie,
" CHALMERS, LE GRAND CHALMERS, FIT MON APOLOGIE!"

 Avis pofthume de Monfieur IRELAND à fon Executeur futur très fidele, touchant l'Ouvrage Apologétique du celebre CHALMERS.—Extrait de quelques Teftamens pretendus Literaires de plufieurs grands Hommes & Gens de Lettres de ce Siecle, en M. S. *chez moi.*

         JASPER HARGRAVE.

COLLECTION THE FIRST.

LONDON:
PRINTED FOR T. BECKET, PALL MALL,
1800.

THE BOOKSELLER

TO

The Readers of the CHALMERIANA.

MESDAMES et MESSIEURS,

IT was once the fate of Horace Walpole, afterwards Earl of Orford, to examine minutely a particular Treatise, though he considered it as " a silly, dull " book, full of blunders and void of facts, in which " the truths were ridiculous and the lies serious, te- " dious in discussion and comic from improbability." These words were certainly prophetic of many late writings, and in my opinion of none more pointedly than of " The Supplemental Apology, and Post- script, for the Believers in the Shakespeare Papers,

by

by George Chalmers." By way of introduction therefore to the CHALMERIANA, (which I have collected for your pleasure and satisfaction,) I shall present you with an Extract from *the Battle of the Books* by Dean Swift, in which I have abridged

THE FABLE

OF

THE BEE AND THE SPIDER.

" Upon the corner of an high window dwelled *a certain* SPIDER, swollen up to the first magnitude by the destruction of an infinite number of *Flies*, whose spoils lay scattered before the gates of his palace, like human bones before the cave of some giant. In this mansion he had dwelt for some time, without danger to his person from *swallows* from above, or to his palace by *brooms* from below. When it was the pleasure of Fortune to conduct thither a wandering BEE, to whose curiosity a broken pane in the glass had discovered itself; and in he went,

went, where expatiating for a while he happened to alight upon one of the outward walls of THE SPIDER's Citadel, which yielding to the unequal weight funk down to the very foundation. While THE BEE was employed in cleanfing his wings, and difengaging them from the ragged remnants of the cobweb, the SPIDER adventured out, when beholding the chafms, the ruins, and the dilapidations of his fortrefs, he was very near at his wit's end He ftormed and fwore like a madman, and having fwelled himfelf into the fize and pofture of a Difputant, began his *argument* in the true fpirit of controverfy, with refolution to be heartily fcurrilous and angry, and fully predetermined in his mind againft all conviction.

" Not to difparage myfelf, faid THE SPIDER, by the comparifon with fuch a —— ; what art thou but a vagabond without houfe or home, without ftock or inheritance? born to no poffeffion of your own, but a pair of wings and a drone-pipe.

Your

Your livelihood is an univerfal plunder upon nature; you are a freebooter over fields and gardens, and for the fake of ftealing, will rob a nettle as readily as a violet. Whereas I am a *domeftic* animal, furnifhed with a *native* ftock within myfelf. This large Caftle, (to fhew my improvements in the mathematics) is all built with my own hands, and the materials *altogether out of my own perfon.*"

" I am glad, anfwered THE BEE, to hear you grant at leaft, that I am come honeftly by my wings and my voice; for then, it feems, I am obliged to heaven alone for my flights and my mufic. I vifit indeed all the flowers and bloffoms of the field and the garden; but whatever I collect from thence enriches myfelf, *without the leaft injury* to their beauty, their fmell, or their tafte. Now for you and your fkill in architecture, and other mathematics, I have little to fay. In that building of yours there might, for ought I know, have been *labour and method* enough, but by woeful experience it is plain,

the

the materials are naught. You boaft indeed of drawing and fpinning out all from yourfelf; yet your inherent portion of *dirt* does not fail of acquifition by *fweepings* exhaled from below; and one infect furnifhes you with a ftore of *poifon* to deftroy another. So that in fhort, the queftion comes all to this; whether is the nobler being of the two, that which by a lazy contemplation of four inches round, by an overweening pride which, feeding and engendering on itfelf, turns all into *excrement and venom*, producing nothing at all but *fly-bane and a cobweb* : or that, which by an univerfal range, with long fearch, much ftudy, true judgment, and diftinction of things, brings home *honey and wax."*

" *The Two Parties of* Books in Arms, (fays the military hiftorian) ftood filent awhile, waiting in fufpence what would be the iffue, which was not long undetermined; for the Bee, grown impatient at fo much lofs of time, fled ftraight away to *a Bed of Rofes*, without waiting for a reply, *and left* the Spider."

Now,

Now, Reader, to the Mufes and JASPER; let us fcent together the morning fragrance on the banks of the Thames and the Avon.

THE BOOKSELLER.

CHALMERIANA:

CHALMERIANA:

OR

A COLLECTION OF PAPERS

LITERARY AND POLITICAL,

ENTITLED,

LETTERS, VERSES, &c.

On reading a late heavy Supplemental Apology for the Believers in the SHAKSPEARE PAPERS, by GEORGE CHARMERS, F. R. S. S. A.

ADDRESSED TO THE EDITOR OF THE MORNING CHRONICLE.

Sept. 4, 1799.

No. I.

EPIGRAM I.

GEORGE, 'tis odd you cannot reft,
Since you rummag'd IRELAND's Cheft:
Think of your Office and your Head—
Sure, you've enough of Scraps and *Lead*!

EPIGRAM

EPIGRAM II.

A DIALOGUE BETWEEN A SCHOOLMASTER AND A *Scholar.*

SCHOOLMASTER.
Master GEORGE, pray, where's your *folio?*

CH——
Octavo, Sir:—Here, here's my Olio *.

SCHOOLMASTER.
What—nought but Blunders? Why, you Goose,
Sure, Bæotia is let loose!
Look, here my Boy: See—Noun, Pronoun—
It must be—Let his Breeches down!
Fault upon fault!—Verb, *Participle* †——

CH——
Oh, dear!—the Rod begins to tickle!

SCHOOLMASTER.
This Adverb's wrong—and this *Conjunction!*

CH——
Pray, Sir, stop:—'tis not my function.

SCHOOLMASTER.
Preposition—Interjection.——

CH——
Spare, and leave me to *reflection.*

---

* Olio—a Dish made by mingling different kinds of Meat.
Dr. JOHNNSON.
† Alluding to Mr. Chalmers's gross Grammatical ignorance in mistaking a Participle for a Verb, and reasoning upon it in the Postcript to his Apology.—The rhyme *Participle* and *tickle*, is, I believe adopted from some *ancient* poet, to whom an allusion is made.
BOOKSELLER.

EPIGRAM III.

THE MINISTER AND THE *Grammarian.*

Says PITT to GEORGE, I like your plan;
    Yet 'tis a little bold:
But he that wins may laugh, my friend;
    I'll turn *your Lead* to Gold!

How many parts has *Income?*——Ten:
    " Sir, *Grammar* has but Eight:"
Why then, next year I'll take your hint;
    Grammar is better for the State.

                  OWEN, Junior.

No. II.

A COLLECTION OF LETTERS, VERSES, &c.

OCCASIONED BY A LATE SUPPLEMENTAL APOLOGY, &c.

To the *EDITOR* of the *MORNING CHRONICLE.*

SIR,   *Inner Temple, Sept.* 8. 1799.

IN confequence of your printing *my* Epigrams in your Paper of 5th September feveral inquifitive perfons have difcovered that I live in the Inner Temple, which I now acknowledge publicly. They have juft fent me a variety of different compofitions in celebration of Mr. Chalmers's immortal Work (which Work every fleeplefs man and woman fhould read), I mean *The Supplemental Apology for the Believers in the Shakefpeare Papers.* The writers all feem to agree in the *weight* of the great Author, and fome of them tell me they fhall tranfmit to my chambers a variety of pleafantries, fuch as Half Odes, fragments of Epiftles, Critical Sketches, and other pieces, which they affure me are *very clever.*

They alfo declare upon the honour of *Poets* (I know you'll laugh), that all their effufions are written out of pure gratitude for the *diverfion* and *merriment* which Mr. C. has afforded them. Perhaps after all, they only banter me.

My

My Clerk has been very angry at paying the poſtage of ſo many Letters from different parts of the kingdom to Mr. Owen, jun. Inner Temple; for, when he expected that ſome of them contained Caſes for me to anſwer, and that others had Retainers, Refreſhing Fees, and ſuch profeſſional douceurs, he found nothing but ſcraps of Poetry and ſuch ſtuff, for which indeed Mr. JASPER HARGRAVE (for that is my Clerk's name) *at preſent* has very little taſte; but he will improve, if I am not miſtaken. He adviſed me either to return them to their reſpective authors, or to ſend them in a lump to the Maſter of the Temple, or the Preacher of Lincoln's-inn, or ſuch folks who know more Greek than Law: but I choſe to be my own maſter in this particular, and ſmiled at my friend Jaſper's want of taſte. But what can one expect from a Copying Clerk? though by the bye, I think they ought to be paid a little better than they are; and I have actually advanced Mr. Jaſper's wages in conſideration of his being obliged to read Verſes now and then, which is the worſt thing a Lawyer can do. It is never forgiven, Sir, in our profeſſion if a man is known to have a turn that way.

I have indeed ſome miſgivings, and fear you may be of my Clerk Jaſper's opinion; yet I have made a ſmall ſelection for you, all in the Epigrammatic way for the preſent, which will be particularly agreeable to a man of taſte like Mr. C. I muſt alſo tell you that I have bought A CHEST (not quite ſo big as Mr. Ireland's) for the purpoſe of keeping all the Verſes, &c. &c. which may be ſent me (and I am threatened with ſo many, that I hope they will be franked:) but the papers will certainly be original; and I can affirm that they never were in the poſſeſſion of any Baronet of ſeven thouſand a year, like the Iriſh Shakeſpeare. I have alſo another cheſt, rather ſmaller, for all
the

the evidences which I have collected concerning *every* writer of Junius: but I have myfelf fome undoubted documents (which have never feen the light), to prove inconteftibly that, after all the difputes on the fubject, JUNIUS and the Author of *The Purfuits of Literature* (I wont tell you yet their real names) *were* BOTH SCOTSMEN. But thefe I fhall referve for the prefent, and begin with the Epigrams, to which the Public, I hope, will pay great attention; but by way of foils I fhall fometimes mix a few of my own.

I am Sir, yours,
OWEN, JUNIOR.

PLUMBO COMMISSA MANEBVNT.

EPIGRAM IV.

A *Chemical* EPIGRAM;
ON READING THE *Supplemental* APOLOGY.

(*Written by Dr.* MOSELEY, *the ingenious Author of the celebrated Treatife on Sugar.*)

SWEET is the Air PITT breathes at Walmer's;
Sweet the Cane in India bred;
Sweet are the *fugar'd* words of CHALMERS;
But his *Sugar* is—*of Lead* !

EPIGRAM

EPIGRAM V.

A *Chimerical* EPIGRAM;

Occasioned by reading the following words in the *Supplemental* Apology, p. 608: " There ought to be no " Comma (,) after (a) *Vacuum*, unless there be one after " (a) *Chimera*."

Written by the Chaplain to the Volunteer Corps of Marshal's Men commanded by Sir James Bland Burgess, Baronet.

Sir JAMES, Knight Marshal in Love's Field,
    Was frighten'd on Cythera,
And *Commas* after Cupid put,
    In dread of his *Chimæra*!

Not so the Knight of Leaden Mace—
    He runs *without a muzzle*,
And tilts at ev'ry Nymph and Grace,
    Content the Cause to puzzle.

To ev'ry Critic in his wrath
    He shews his Gorgon head:
A *Vacuum* is all he fears—
    So fills the void with *Lead!*

EPIGRAM

EPIGRAM VI.

A *Nautical* EPIGRAM.

(*Signed in the* MS. EVAN NEPEAN, *Secretary to the Admiralty.*) J. H.

Great DUNCAN late off Camper-down
   A *Supplemental* Pilot wifh'd,
What time he ftrengthen'd England's Crown,
   And the Dutchmen deftly *difh'd*.

What man of *weight* fhould be preferr'd,
   Whifpers around the Council ran:
PORTLAND humdrumm'd, DUNDAS demurr'd,
   But none had wit to name the man.

Says SPENCER, thoughtful, fhrewd, and cool,
   " You have a *Clerk* of folid head;
" Send *Him*, my Lord of LIVERPOOL;
   " For who can better heave *the Lead?*"

(A true Copy)
(L. S.)   JASPER HARGRAVE,
   Clerk to Mr. Owen, jun. Inner Temple.

No. III.

To the EDITOR *of the* MORNING CHRONICLE.

SIR, *Inner Temple, Sep.* 13. 1799.

MY Friend and clerk, Mr. JASPER HARGRAVE, to whom I introduced you lately, and with whom I hope you will soon be better acquainted, is very solicitous that I should employ him again in *your* service. I say in yours, not mine; for since I have given him free access to the Poetical Chest, I can get very little work done in my office. Yet the dog, who scarce ever heard of wit before, now attempts raillery himself, and assures me his Work is still in *Banco Regis*, with this difference, that all he does now is in the name of GEORGE C. instead of GEORGE R.; and, what with Demurrers, Replications and Rejoinders, Rebutters and Sur-rebutters, which he puts in rhyme, he teazes me out of all patience, and then swears with Horace, whom he has heard me cite, that Apollo has saved *him*. However, as Jasper writes so legible a hand, I must look over these little impertinences.

He

He is so taken with the contents of the numerous packets which I receive every day, that he never leaves me a moment in quiet: with a significant look he is constantly coming to me with Verses—" Pray, Sir, let me copy this Epigram—this Fragment (you see whose it is;—mum); but above all, the beginning of this Epistle—I'm sure it would suit Mr. Editor, who is a judge of fine writing." It is in vain for me to cry out, " Hold your tongue, Jasper: don't you see I am employed in answering *an Income Case* for Mr. LOWNDES of the Tax Office, and can't speak to you." But nothing can stop Jasper. It is no wonder the Commissioners should now and then be puzzled, when I am entrusted to give opinions on the Act. I sometimes swear, and wish Mr. LOWNDES would let Jasper put the whole Income Act in Verse, and select the essence of it in *Golden Rules*, for the Commercial Commissioners to print and distribute. They would have such an effect in the City! There is not a Banker or a West India Merchant who would not feel the force of this decimal, or rather decimating arithmetic in Verse. Dictæ per Carmina fortes, Mr. Editor, they say; and there is indeed a necessity for some *charm* to draw men of business to speak out fairly and honestly.

The other day in the middle of a *Declaration* Jasper was copying (and I was writing an opinion in the next room), he came in very unseasonable haste, and said he wanted to go out immediately, and could not rest till he had been. I remonstrated, and said, " You know Mr. Mingay expects me to read the very case at seven this evening, and it absolutely must be finished." No; all in vain: he would go out.—" But where do you want to go, Jasper?" " To Mr. Hookham's Sir, for the *Supplemental Apology*, GEORGE C. in the Case of IRELAND and Co. But it is difficult at present

present to settle *all* the points in dispute between George and Ireland!" Jasper gave me a sly look, and affected to whisper.—" But why so hasty?" " Sir, I want the words in evidence, and think besides, that I shall be able to make a note or two upon a Fragment of Lord C—le's which contains something *mysterious*, and particularly as there is no *print* or *drawing* annexed to it, to tell what his Lordship means, which is very convenient in *Dramatic* performances, which might be otherwise unintelligible. It came in the last packet, and I have set my mind upon decyphering his Lordship's meaning." By the bye, I should have told you, Mr. Editor, that Jasper had not yet seen the Supplemental Apology, and knew it only by character and as I had informed him. In short, I let him go.

When he got to Bond-street, he was so sublimely intent on his poetry, that the Duke of Queensbury had like to have run over him in his *new Piccadilly Cart*,* and if Lord William had not fortunately seized the reins and stopt the horse, I should probably have lost Jasper's services for several weeks. I wish all those *young* fellows who drive in Bond-street would take a little more care of the Ladies and the poets. The other day, as the dashing Brewer and Madame were driving furiously at the turning, Wright the bookseller had nearly lost poor Gifford, whose eyes are none of the best, as he was crossing the street and thinking of his Juvenal.—But this you must read in a parenthesis.

When Jasper came to the shop," Mr. Hookham," says he, " I want one of your *Circulating* Books—Mr. George Chalmers's

---

* It is hoped that the Duke's Coachmaker has preserved a drawing of this elegant Summer vehicle in *September* for the instruction of posterity, concerning this young Damasippus. *Incolumem præstet Septembribus horis.*

BOOKSELLER.

mers's Supplemental Apology; but I want to keep it a month or six weeks." Mr. Hookham replied, in his usual vein of pleasantry (you know Hookham's manner, Mr. Editor, it is universally admired, quite a pattern for his profession, and I should have told you, that he and Jasper are old friends). " You are jocular, my good friend; a *circulating* book! I see you have been at Debrett's in your way to pick up a little wit. Bless your heart, *Circulating* Apology!—why, man, it never moves; it is absolutely fixed to the counter at Egerton's. Between friends, I think George should write another volume as large, to apologise for the *manner* of writing it. It was not ill judged in Mr. C. to publish it at the *Military* Library, and the bookseller himself a military man." " Happy, happy, happy pair!—none but the *brave* deserve, &c." You know, Hookham is Musical; and there was something inexpressibly arch in his eye when he hummed the air: you would have thought he had sold fifty Concert Tickets that morning. He then said, " To be fair with you, my friend Jasper, I have really but one copy of it: the facts I am told, are all fiction and invention.— a mere clumsy Irish novel; and some say it is a horrible large (you know what) in octavo: but it is of indispensable use to me in the Reading room; so you cannot have it; 'faith, you cannot."—" But I must take it with me for a week at least," said Jasper hastily: " No, no, you cannot; but you are so good-natured, you wont press me when you know what I want it for. Some of the visitors are so d—mned fond of newspapers, and keep them so long, that many of my subscribers cannot get a paper sometimes without waiting an hour. So I contrive to keep the Supplemental Apology constantly on the table, and as I have it bound very fine, it acts like a metallic tractor, and draws Dr. H. Dr. R. Mr. L. Mr. K. and some others who keep the papers insufferably long. However when they once get hold of it

for

for a few minutes, they are foon difqualified for all other reading whatfoever, and become as faft and fixed to their chairs as the Lady in Comus. You may be fure I do not fend for Sabrina on the occafion. The apology itfelf is indeed the true effence of Nepenthe mixed with a very large proportion of the Extract of Saturn. My bookbinder has ornamented the back and fides of the Supplement with all the emblems of the Saturnian age, and has contrived to ftamp Saturn's crown and leaden mace, of which Jupiter deprived him, and the *rude* fcythe which he was forced to take up with afterwards, when he could do no better. My binder has a pretty tafte for mythology, Mr. Jafper." Hookham was proceeding on the fubject in as *neat and appropriate a fpeech* as if he were going to prefent a pair of colours in petticoats, but Jafper was impatient, and would ftay no longer. However, as he was determined to have the Supplemental Apology at any rate, he went to Egerton's and bought it, like an A double S.

Jafper then told me, it would have done any humane man good to have witneffed the rapture of Mr. Egerton, when he actually *took the money for the book*. He could hardly believe that any man in his fenfes would part with feven fhillings for fuch a *thing*, and feemed to think it a kind of miracle. He told Jafper in confidence all the propofals he had received from the undertaker, the trunk-maker, and the coffee-houfe, if he would part with *the whole at once*, in fheets. But (as I know, Mr. Editor, you will be filent on the occafion) he at laft told my Clerk Jafper, as a profound State-fecret, that no lefs a perfonage than General Sir Ralph Abercromby had been with him a few days before he fet out on the fecret expedition to Holland, to treat. " Good God, Mr. Egerton, to treat—about what?" faid Jafper in furprife. " I'll tell you, if you will but have a moment's patience, my good friend. Sir Ralph faid he had it in command to treat

with

with me for *the whole* impression, and offered to take it off my hands en masse, and ship it in casks as *sheet-lead*, in case of any deficiency, or if they should have *a little more to do than they expected*, (which will sometimes happen in the best appointed schemes) it was his intention to use them rolled up instead of bullets against the Dutchmen. An Officer who was with Sir Ralph, who had heard of the fame of *all* Mr. Chalmers's writings, laughed at the idea of *sheet*-lead, and as he spoke French admirably, said, " *Ah, vous avez raison, Monsieur le General, c'est étre fort prévoyant; mais c'est plutot* DU PLOMB EN BARRE *que les feuilles de ce Monsieur Chalmers.*" But Mr. Egerton, for some reason or other, declined this *Government* proposal, and I believe has heartily repented of it ever since.

Mr. Editor, if ever you wish to make a man useful to you, and keep him so, put all books and verses out of his way. The effect they have already had on my Clerk Mr. Jasper Hargrave, is prodigious and alarming, and very inconvenient to me. He insensibly has acquired (you know I hinted to you that I thought he would) a kind of taste, and thinks himself qualified for something better than copying. He takes upon himself to judge, and for the present I would observe that if you do not quite approve all the verses I send, I verily believe he puts in a verse or two of his own, which he thinks has a *finer* effect. But I must submit, as I have made him what he is, by my own folly.

It will be your own fault if I do not send you an account of Jasper's progress in the fine arts; and the books he reads and the criticisms he makes on men and manners. He had the assurance the other day to tell me, he should " *leave all meaner things* ;" and when I told him to give over such nonsense, and talk about *the three goats* in the Welsh cause

I was

I was retained in, he feized his military hat, (for Jafper belongs to our Temple Corps; he is rather a fmart fellow—I'll point him out to you fome day in our Gardens), and cocking it as gallantly as Capt. Graham himfelf, faid, "Together let us beat this ample field; try"—" Try firft to hold your filly tongue, Jafper," I faid, " this poetical cheft has turned your head, and I fear the Supplemental Apology will finifh the bufinefs." But as he is a good humoured fellow, he only fmiled, " You fhall fee, Sir." Upon my word he is a more fingular character than you would expect; it is a pity he fhould blufh unfeen, like the flower of the poet. But from all the fymptoms I have obferved, and perhaps may tell you in a future letter, my Clerk Jafper is irrecoverably a verfe-man and a profe-man. I cannot fancy you will think I have faid too much of him.

I fhall in my next give you fome extracts from the cheft, which Jafper is now copying in his faireft hand. Mr. Chalmers has appeared in the literary circle in London, like Vulcan among the celeftials on Mount Olympus. When that aukward God came hobbling and limping to offer them *his fervices*, Homer tells us, that " inextinguifhable laughter burft forth among the immortal Gods," or, as I think Dacier fays, they indulged " en grands eclats de rire á gorge deployée." But it is high time now to prefent you with the felection for this day, of the original verfes fuggefted by the fupplemental profe of the Anglo-Lemnian. Jafper has written them very plain indeed. One copy he felected himfelf; I need not tell you which; you will poffibly guefs.

I am yours truly,
Owen, Junior.

P. S. I am very forry indeed, that contrary to my expectations,

pectations, you must wait for the Epigrams till my next Number. Jasper is not ready, for he made so large a blot on his paper, that he chose to copy the whole over again; for he's a neat creature. But I rather suspect he has been exercising what he calls his judgment, and I fear has put in a line of two, and will bring them to me with an air of triumph, and swear that " The verse divine comes mended from his pen."

No.

No. IV.

To the EDITOR *of the* MORNING CHRONICLE.

SIR, *Inner Temple, Sept.* 21, 1799.

IF my Clerk, Mr. JASPER HARGRAVE, continues to give such pleasant accounts as he did lately of his conversation with Hookham and Egerton on the *Supplemental* Apology, I find my Chambers will soon be little better than a Lounge for young Lawyers. I believe no less than ten or twelve of them knocked at my door the day after I sent you my last Letter, not to see me, but Jasper. Now, Sir, if a Book, or a Sermon, or a Poem of real merit comes out, these young fellows have seldom time to read them; but they still keep up the old character of our Inns of Court: they study Shakespeare, d—mn the Commentators and their lumber, parody the characters, send you a few squibs for your CHRONICLE, then dress (if it can be called dressing at present), dine at Richards's, stroll to the Play at half price—and you may guess how the evening ends. These young Knights Templars are not quite so alarmed at

Cupid

Cupid and his Mama as our friend Sir James, " Knight Marshal in Love's Field," as the Cyprian Chaplain of his amiable Corps styled him in the Epigram, which Jasper copied for you in my second Number. But, to do them justice, nothing suits them so well as a neat Epigram; for wit, you know, is easier understood than law.

However, if they call so often, I shall give you an account of their characters, as they take up too much of my Clerk's time. But as I remember most of them at College, I shall let them have their way at present. They often say to me; " OWEN, where did you pick up that Clerk of yours? he is a lively odd dog; shrewd and communicative. Why, he can't be above two and-twenty at most: he's something of a Quiz, but we don't like to banter him too much, for he generally gives us something better than we bring ; that's the truth of it."

" You must do as you please, Gentlemen ; but, upon my word I cannot spare you my own time any more than Gibbs or Erskine; and, if you knew the extent of Jasper's ideas, perhaps you would be a little more considerate of his. If he jokes with you, however, he'll always do it like a Gentleman ; he'll never dismiss you in a rude, coarse, clumsy way, but only hint at the improvement young men like you might make of your time and *talents*; and, if his manner of pronouncing a word now and then stands instead of an epithet, you'll excuse him."

We talk in this manner, but curiosity will get the better of propriety. Yet for my own part, I never saw any thing succeed well without a little ceremony, and the most perfect good manners. The habit of asking questions, and teasing people in that way, is the rudest custom imaginable:

no Gentleman ever indulges it. I said one day to them—
" Pray, why is a Letter sealed? and why does a man not
put his name to a book?" As they are most of them
men of education, they understood me. But Jasper said
rather briskly, " Leave them alone, Sir," (for Jasper begins
to feel his consequence,) " and I'll answer for it, that Mr.
Owen Junior's Chambers in the Inner Temple will soon be
known *par excellence* as *Le Bureau des Ouvrages d'Esprit.*"
" Yes, my good friend; but, pray, how am I to live in the
mean time?" " Live, Sir!—oh, I'll tell you: the easiest
thing in nature." (Jasper by the bye, is the strangest fellow for leaving things to *Nature* I ever saw). " Pray,
how?" " Get another set of Chambers, Sir, and leave
these to Ireland, Chalmers, the Muses and Jasper. Never
blend these matters: the Thames water by our garden
will never mix with Castalia. Sure, you havn't got any
nonsensical *Tunnel* under Mount Parnassus in your head?
why zounds, you might as well think of conveying wit and
salt water from Brighton under ground together to Lambeth
by act of Parliament?" " Don't be severe, Jasper; learn to
respect the Gazette, the Church and the House. I want
to see no *Sergeant at Mace* under my roof but my old friend
Leaden George." But my Clerk began to be more violent;
he talked of raptures *firing* and visions *blessing* him, and
cried out, " I feel, I feel"——" That you're a d—mned
fool, Jasper: but, as my uncle has left me a few hundreds,
I will take another set, and leave Paper-buildings to you
and Daines Barrington; and let me tell you, I wish you or
any *Student* there may put your learning, ingenuity, and
researches to half as good a purpose for yourself and your
country as that excellent and respectable man has done all
his life." My Clerk shook his head.

I have

I have told you *all* this, Mr. Editor, becaufe I promifed to conceal nothing from you: but, as the relation of a man's private domeſtic affairs is, of all things, the moſt tedious, infufferable, and uninterefting to other people, you will feldom hear any more of me, but as I am connected with Jafper, who now ſtudies night and day. But he fays he has made one refolution, which is, to read no languages but Latin, French, and Englifh, which he thinks it a fhame for any Gentleman not to know, if he has opportunity. To be fure at prefent Jafper's Latin is not very deep, nor is his reading too methodical. He is a Divine, a Phyfician, a Lexicographer, and all things by turns, as his whim directs.

The other day (you may imagine my furprife) he came to me, and faid, " Well, Sir, I've found out the reafon why Chalmers wrote his Supplemental Apology for Shakefpeare in octavo. But without knowing Latin I fhould have known nothing of the matter. Look here, Sir, what a fingular coincidence!—George C. is a fcholar in *his* way." To my aftonifhment, what book fhould he produce but Mr. Daubeny's Appendix to his Guide to the Church in two volumes." " Merciful Heaven." faid I— " a Guide to the Church! What can that have to do with Chalmers and Shakefpeare?"—" Every thing, Sir, now-a-days has to do with Shakefpeare: the difficulty is, to find out what has not to do with him." " But, Jafper, you're tedious." " Oh, Sir, faid he, my bufinefs is only with the Preface; I have not read a line of the work; it's out of my way: I leave that to Mr. Wilberforce and Hannah. Only look at thefe Latin words: George Chalmers muſt have read them (Good Heaven, how ufeful Latin is!) either here or in Erafmus himfelf; OCTAVUM
OCCUPER

occupent apologiæ!" " Well, Jafper; what then?"
" Why, don't you fee, Sir, it is the decided opinion of Erafmus, according to the beft tranflation of him, that *"All* apologies *fhould be written* in octavo!" " That's rather a
moot point," I faid in my law jargon: " but let me fee:
perhaps Chalmers's knowledge of Latin and yours is pretty
much alike." I took the book and read the context, and
then burft out a laughing: " You filly jackanapes, if the
Emigrant Abbé who teaches you French performs his
part as well as the Scotch Profeffor who *grounds* you
in Latin, you'll make a hopeful progrefs in the tongues.
But you are a wit, Jafper, certainly you are a wit. Don't
you fee Erafmus complains that the *eighth volume* of the
collection of his Works muft confift of Apologies, and
concludes, like George Chalmers, " What a *wretch* am
I!" or *Me Miferum*! Now the difference, among a few
other points, between Erafmus of Rotterdam and George of
Bœotia is this, that every thick volume which George
writes will at leaft require eight volumes of Apologies as
thick; and of this George muft be fenfible by this time. So
much for *your Latin*, Jafper. Don't expofe yourfelf, like
George, to the Critics and the Public.

" But, come; give me the Epigrams you have copied:
perhaps they may make fome amends for your Law Latin.
You do write an excellent hand; that muft be allowed:
and it is very ufeful when a Writer can keep the Editor, the
Printer, and the Compofitor all in good humour; he need not
then give himfelf much trouble about *the Devil* and **G.C.**"
Jafper, who was a little confounded at his miftake, put the
Epigrams in my hand, and for the firft time fince I have
known him, was a little out of countenance. " Cheer
up, Jafper," I faid, " your betters in the King's Bench,
                                                    and

and other places, make miſtakes of this kind every day, when they will quote Latin, and appear learned. To be ſure you do write a fine round text. Look at it, Mr. Editor,

I am your's truly,

OWEN, Junior.

EPIGRAMS *(continued)*

ON THE HEAVY SUPPLEMENTAL APOLOGY.

"*Plumbo Commiſſa Manebunt.*"

EPIGRAM VII.

A *Libitinal* EPIGRAM.

(Signed in the original M. S. T. JARVIS, Patent Coffin Maker, oppoſite the King on the Black Horſe, Charing Croſs.   JASP. H.)

When DYER gave the world his FLEECE,
    He ſoon grew wond'rous ſullen;
For every Wit pronounc'd, his Muſe
    Would buried be in woollen.

Oh,

Oh, had poor DYER yet surviv'd,
   CHALMERS had made him proud,
And o'er the Bard and Sheep had thrown
   His *Supplemental* shrowd.

Lin'd with his book's metallic leaves,
   What could disturb the dead?
Secure, when all without was Wool,
   And all within was *Lead*.

EPIGRAM VIII.

A *Ceremonious* EPIGRAM.

(The original M. S. is signed in a very gentlemanly handwriting, STEPHEN COTTRELL, Kt. Master of the Ceremonies, &c. &c.   JASP. H.)

"Laws *without manners** are but vain,"
   The Swan of Tiber sung;
And from Venusium to Blackheath
   The polish'd echo rung.

"Laws, *manners*, graces, what are they,
   "Or all that HORACE saith?"
Cries GEORGE; since *Ireland* boasts, I stand
   Defender of the Faith!

---

* *Manners*, in the plural, signifies *studied civility.*— Johnson's Dictionary. But Mr. CHALMERS always uses it in the singular throughout the whole Supplemental Apology.   JASP. H.

EPIGRAM IX.

A *Virtuous* Epigram.

Recommended to every Bachelor in the Kingdom; occasioned by reading the following affectionate Aphorism by GEORGE CHALMERS, A.S.S, in two parts, the second of which is beautifully ambiguous, viz. " *Men* " *usually make love to women; and* (Ambigitur) *woe* " *them to wed.*"

Supplemental Apology, page 96.

(N.B. The M.S. in the original is signed GEORGE COLMAN *the Younger*. JASP. H.)

GEORGE to the critic camp repairs,
　And turns poetic suttler,
Then *reasons* on the bills he brings
　From Gilbert, Locke and Butler.

Queen BESS he calls a buxom maid,
　Next *proves* it by a sonnet,
That SHAKESPEARE threw the handkerchief,
　And she look'd sweetly on it.

But

But since " to women men make love,
  " And woo them *(for†)* to wed;"
Bess would have chang'd Will's mulb'rry rod
  For George's *Mace of Lead.*

† Grammar, sense, and the harmony of the verse require the insertion of this *causal* or *conjugal* article.
    Jasp. H. from the Grammatical Canons of
     George Chalmers.

(A True Copy. From the Originals preserved in Mr. Owen, Junior's, Chambers in the Inner Temple.

(L.S.)   Jasper Hargrave,
    Clerk to Mr. Owen, Junior.)

No. V.

To the EDITOR *of the* MORNING CHRONICLE.

SIR, *Inner Temple, Sept.* 26.

IN compliance with the requeſt of my Clerk, Mr. JASPER HARGRAVE, I have taken a new ſet of Chambers for myſelf, and left him in full poſſeſſion of Paper Buildings. My Chambers are dull enough, but Jaſper's are indeed very pleaſant, and command a fine view of the Surry Hills, the bridges, boats, and the volunteers in our garden, and in ſhort of every thing which gives the idea of pleaſure, plenty, and ſecurity in a country. They are now ſacred to Ireland, Chalmers, the Muſes, and Jaſper. I called there this morning, and rather alarmed him: " I hope, Sir," ſaid Jaſper, " there is no Writ of Ejectment: Poets and their Clerks muſt have a fixed habitation, the higher the better, or they can do nothing. Sure they don't envy us the Temple. It is time enough to think about Elyſium, where Virgil tells us that Poets and other

great

great men have no houses over their heads, but are always lounging from one meadow to another, or lolling over a bank or a river, and never mntion a word about pen and ink." " I suppose, Jasper, you'll shew me the case in Dryden's Mantuan Reports, *temp. August. Imp. A. U. C.* 734, *Sextil. V. Sagitt. Occident. N. P.* But, pooh, man, you are safe: the Benchers have signed the Lease of the Chambers, and Daines Barrington, who was present at the sealing, with his usual pleasantry and happiness of allusion to the old Kalendar, added significantly; Pray tell my friend Jasper from me, (as I hear he reads Latin), ' LYRA *cras non occidet, ex edicto Julii.*' So here you shall be fixed as long as you like it, and continue to do your business with assiduity and attention." Jasper bowed with complacency.

" But, pray what are you reading?" I looked, and saw he had got the *fourth* book of *The Dunciad* open before him, which, though it spoils the integrity and plan of the Poem, certainly contains some of the neatest points and very best poetry. Jasper, who had not quite recovered his confusion from the Latin blunder I told you of in my last Letter, said; " You see, a Lawyer's Clerk may have now and then some sense of propriety; so I have got an English book on my table; and, depend upon it, I shall study Latin a little more before I quote it again, or I shall be as ridiculous as *Leaden* George himself, and make as many *blunders* as he has done, and then have nothing to do but to make Apologies for them. By the bye, you know George's definition of *a Blunderbuss*, don't you? It is conceived with infinite wit and great *vivacité de pesanteur*, as my French
Abbé

Abbe fays." "No; I don't know it." "Then I'll tell you, Sir; 'I call any writer a *Blunderbufs*,' fays Leaden George, 'who fcribbles *blunderingly**.' Who fhall fay that George is drowfy or heavy? To be fure George generally miffes fire with his Blunderbufs; but then he knocks you down in the politeft manner imaginable with the but end of it." "Very well, Jafper, you improve: but from the united labours of a French Emigrant and a Scotch Profeffor, much literary advantage may be expected *in time*; only wait."

"Yes, Sir," faid Jafper: "but I ftudy Latin very hard at night; and in a week or two I am to read Horace, and try my hand at a *tranflation*." "Indeed?" "Even fo, Sir; and Profeffor Mac Taggart, of Aberdeen, my tutor in the *Humainities*, flatters me I fhall fucceed as well as fome others have done lately, and thinks I may be put *in the Commiffion*." "*Commiffion*, for what, Jafper?— What can Profeffor Mac Taggart mean?—*not for preferving the peace* at Horace's Farm, I'm fure, where it is all confufion at prefent, and the Sabine folks thereabouts fwear that his fwans are turned into geefe, gabbling and cackling in fuch a manner that you can't tell one note from another. They add alfo, that, if Horace were alive again, and were to put on his boots and *ride on horfeback* round his grounds and premifes, he would not find a fingle thing as he left it, but *tranflated* from one place to another in fuch a way that it would be impoffible for him to know what was his own. But they fay it was all the fault of *Auguftus and his Minifter*, who drew up the Leafe in favour of Horace in fuch binding terms, that it never could

---

* Supplemental Apology, page 601.

could be made over to any other perfon whatever." Jafper looked a little blank. " Courage, my friend: I mean no reflexion on your ability," I replied. " But only, don't be in fuch a hurry to *gallop* over Horace's grounds. It's true enough, ' *Optat ephippia* Bos;' afk Profeffor Mac Taggart the meaning of thofe words, as foon as you come to the fatires; leave them for the prefent. You do copy moft admirably; but you have not yet done enough for me to afford you the Falernian; and let me add, it is much eafier to manage the *cooperage* at Somerfet Houfe, than to draw off the true vintage from the old Sabine cafks. In a month or two you fhall try your hand at an ode; but never expect to hold of MECENAS *in capite* in this country: take my word for it. At prefent copy on; can't you be contented with being *ufeful?*" " There is fome truth in that, (faid Jafper) I thank you."

We chatted a little on poetry in general, and the fubject of the French Abbe's leffons; I faid, " Some of the Emigrants have publifhed very pretty editions of their claffics, Racine, La Fontaine, and fo on; and upon my word I think that is *all the good they do here*; but that is not your bufinefs now; all I have to fay, LET US MIND OUR FRENCH. Hey, Jafper?" " Time enough, Sir, for politics, we fhall come to them in good time: but now to the Epigrams. I really admire an Epigram as much as you do; but why nothing elfe? *Jovis omnia plena*: look at the cheft: here is an admirable choice; why fhould you confine me? Here is laurel, and myrtle, with a rofe tree now and then, and jeffamine; leaves, bloffoms, flowers, all from Apollo's own garden, true fprigs and flips that will grow, (faid Jafper.) What fignifies fitting always at the foot of the mountain, when fo many flowers grow on the

fides,

sides, and goodly trees on the top?" "You're quite in raptures, Jasper, I believe I must give you a *declaration to draw*, and take down your plethora a little. You speak too slightingly of an Epigram. To what purpose have you been reading the fourth book of the Dunciad, which is open at the very lines I could have wished." "Where, Sir?" "Alter only a word or two, and we have these—

"We've reach'd the work; the all that mortal can;
South had beheld *that master-piece of man.*"

—" Why, Sir, this may be true, and Dr. South is good authority, and they say it is the *ne plus ultra* of a Westminster man, at least the young fellows, who frequent my chambers, tell me so. But, Sir, I've another objection," says Jasper. " What is that, my friend?" " I grant, Mr. Owen, that the great authors of these epigrammatic sallies have enlivened the public at GEORGE's expence. It must, indeed, be extremely pleasant to be the cause of wit in other men. But be a little cautious, Sir, GEORGE C. may ' make a Star Chamber matter of it*.' I know he has been reading deeply of late about ' Robert Shallow, Esq. Justice of Peace, and *Coram*,' F. R. S. and A. double S. He has been known to declare with Slender, that ' all his successors, gone before him, have done so; and his ancestors that come after, may.'

" George, you know, has a gift for *Chronology*. He can tell the day *when* Shakespeare *first* made love to Queen Elizabeth, and where the assignation was made;—he knows the day *when* Heminge the Actor altered a clause in his will in favour of one of his first cousins, when he had originally intended

---

Merry Wives of Windsor. Act I.

intended it for an aunt, who, as it appears from a M.S. in poffeffion of Mr. Malone, had offended him;—he knows *when* old Dennis took a dofe of phyfic, in confequence of a fatire of Mr. Pope;—he knows the day *when* Lord Liverpool *firſt* came into notice on the fhoulders of Lord Chatham, not of Lord Bute, and can tell you *when* the Scotch intereſt began to decline in this Country (which is faid to be his *maſter-piece*). But George is defperately fond of all the *Predicaments, when, where, how,* &c. &c. and once took a few leſſons from old Lord Monboddo, who foon turned him off in a paſſion, as he did not underſtand a word of Greek. But what I think his beſt difcovery is this—he knows the year, the month, and the very day of the month, *when* ' Greene (actually) fold his *Groat's-worth of Wit,*' though he did not live to publiſh it *himſelf*; and that " Henry Chettle *performed that fervice* for the *real*† Author.' George diſtinguiſhes nicely between Publiſhers, Authors, and Bookſellers; Mr. Bayes's dance of the Sun and Moon in Eclipſe, in the *Rehearſal,* is the very picture of George's *judgment*." " But what do you think of his *wit*, friend Jafper?" " Think?—why I think that if George had only the twentieth part of Green's *wit*, who, it feems, had but a groat's-worth upon the whole, he never would have publiſhed that d—mn'd ſtupid *Apology*." " But, Jaſper, you forget: he never *fold* it, like Greene." " No, no, my friend;—*fold* it?—That's another ſtory. *Sold* it, indeed?—No: Egerton's a cunning little Iſaac; fhrewd, fhrewd. No, no, I fay: he's not fuch a fool as to *buy* George's wit—it is enough to publiſh it; though George does *wear brown hair* like Mrs. Anne Page, and ' fometimes fpeaks *ſmall* like a woman;' which is the true reading

---

† Supplemental Apology, page 272.

ing of the paffage from the folio of 1623."—" That may be, Jafper: but, to your bufinefs."

He replied, "Yes, Sir, but pray confent to my deferring the Epigrams for a week or two at leaft. Do look here. The cheft is fo full, that if I were to copy with all the diligence of Wallace and Troward's Firft Clerk, I fhould have enough to do for the whole winter. Let us have a little variety. Befides, Sir, the compofitions are coming in every day; you muft get me a *fupplemental* cheft, or I fhall be all in confufion. Pray do, and I think I fhall be able to arrange the papers, and fupply Mr. Editor with a number or two every week, if he likes to have them." " I can't tell what to fay to that laft point, Jafper; but if you will continue to be diligent, I'll try what can be done." He then put a paper of verfes into my hand which he thought you and I fhould approve. " What are they, Jafper? if there is no impropriety, and you will promife to copy them out in your very beft round text, I will confent." " They are in point, and about the Shakefpeare folks, Sir, quite in character, I like the verfes myfelf." " That may be Jafper, I don't care much what they are about, if they are good."

But Mr. Editor, you may depend upon it, *Nunquam nifi dextro tempore.* . . . You will underftand this, Sir, without the help of Jafper's Latin Tutor in the *Humainities*, Profeffor Mac Taggart of Aberdeen. In a few days, I believe, I fhall fend you my Clerk's choice, if I fhould approve it; I almoft think we may truft him: but from fome late events, I am not inclined to truft *any* man implicitly, and never more than is abfolutely neceffary.

Your's truly,
OWEN, Junior.
No.

No. VI.

———

To the EDITOR *of the* MORNING CHRONICLE.

SIR,   *Inner Temple, Oct.* 4, 1799.

I acquainted you in my laſt, that I ſhould probably preſent you with ſome Verſes from the Cheſt, of JASPER's own choice, if I approved them, in conſideration of his diligence and daily improvement. But, before he put them into my hand, Jaſper came to me rather in a hurry; " Sir, I forgot to tell you that I have a long introduction in proſe to the Poetry, and it is very learned indeed; but I thought it was too long to copy, and beſides I could not. Will you believe it, Sir? There are ſome citations in Arabic, one or two in the Hindoo from the Aſiatic Reſearches, and Greek without end. As for the Latin, I am not much afraid of it, and with Profeſſor Mac Taggart nothing is to be deſpaired of."—" Is it meant as a new Arabian Night's Entertainment juſt tranſlated, Jaſper?" I replied. " Sir, I cannot tell; but as I think you have no ſkill yourſelf in Oriental matters, and never had *an Antelope's ſkin round your neck*, pray ſhall I ſend

it

it to Dr. Joseph White at Oxford, or stop Professor Carlisle before he goes to the Seraglio at Constantinople? With the Hindoo, Persic, and Chinese I shall have little trouble, as Major Ousely and the deeply learned and most ingenious Mr. Henley are at hand; and if a Manuscript were to be sent from the new *Alexandrian* Library just discovered in the polished city of Tombuctoo, the African Association would lend us *their* Dictionary. There is no difficulty now in decyphering any tongue. I will trust the Greek with you."

"You are very obliging, Jasper; you are pleasantly sarcastic, and seem to have as fine a notion of LUMPING, as if you had taken lessons from a certain great master in that art in the House of Commons. But what is it about?"—"It seems to be about *Parody*, Sir, which this Dissertator, whenever I can understand him, declares to be something above burlesque or farce, and that it may be serious, satirical, or jocular. Then comes an Arabic citation, which not being understood, the Author, I suppose, imagined would have great weight with your honour."—"I am glad to see you read Swift, Master Jasper; but do proceed without these reasons of your's." "The writer, Sir, next refers to the *Margites* of Homer."—"I did not think he had been such a fool, Jasper: what signifies talking of non-entities, and making *proofs* out of them?"—"That, Sir, may be convenient sometimes," said Jasper significantly; mock Doctors always talk in this way, when they would convince a patient."—"But what is this about *Parody*, Jasper?"—"Why, Sir, you stopt me: let me see; I left off about Margites: the writer then talks of raillery, and the sublime, the genius of wit, and the art of removing Larvæ from certain writers, and taking off their masque. Then follow some observations about the original meaning of an

ænigma,

ænigma, and a *barbarism*, according to the ancients. Here is some Greek from Aristotle, Sir, I wish you would construe it to me. After a great deal of matter, too long to transcribe, or even to read at present, the Dissertator suddenly turns to the composition of a celebrated Parodist of antiquity, one MATRON; I think the name, Sir, is *Matron;* pray, look at the M. S."—" It is, Jasper: but do go on."—" Why, Sir, he says, that Matron's description of an Attic feast in the Homeric manner, is one of the happiest and earliest effusions of this kind *upon record*; it has much point and grace. The M.S. then cites the case in *Athenæus*, B. iv.; but that is in your Honour's way, and quite out of mine; give me Phillips's SPLENDID SHILLING."—On the mention of Shillings in these hard times, Jasper contrived to fling in a hint about raising the wages of Lawyers Copying Clerks; and I was sorry that several of the eminent Solicitors I know were not present, that they might be induced to do as I have done. The Copying Clerks in Somerset-place and the Post-office, and indeed in all the public offices, might also be considered with great justice.

In conclusion, I said; " Well, Jasper, you have run over part of the contents of this M.S. in a shambling kind of way; but what is the signature to this packet of prose?" —" I think Sir," said Jasper, " it is a pity that so much ingenuity should be lost to the world (though I have left out above two thirds even of the abridgment of it), but here are only initials, and those are blotted horribly; I cannot decide whether they are R. P—n, C. B—y, S.H—y, or St. W—n, for the life of me. The Verses are signed plainly, W. G—d, though, if they had not been so plain, I should have assigned them to the veteran *Arthur*."— " But, give me the verses, Jasper; you are right: Dissertations fertations are too long for our friend Mr. Editor; but we may offer him the fubftance of them. If there is any fragment, why he may have that, as it is in the cheft." " Provided there is no Greek in it, Sir."—" You are right again, Jafper: but, what are the Verfes about?" Sir, they are a Parody on that celebrated patriotic compofition called HOSIER'S GHOST, by Leonidas Glover. We all know the hiftory of that brave but unfortunate Admiral; and the Parodift feems to think that the literary fate of poor CAPELL, the Editor of Shakefpeare, refembles it in many points, when the imagination of a Poet is fet at work in adapting it.

" The Ghoft of CAPELL appears to congratulate Edmund Malone, Efq. on his victory over IRELAND, and *Leaden* GEORGE; but feems to think that though Shakefpeare wanted no vindication, Capell does. Befides, Ghofts and Shades are all the fafhion now."— " So they have been from the time of Homer, my friend Jafper, and always will be, when they are called up for a good purpofe, to ferve our country, and the caufe of virtue, or to inflict righteous vengeance againft public delinquents!"—" Very true, Mr. Owen; but in this parody here is frefh water inftead of falt, though a man may be drowned as effectually in a river as in the South Sea." —" You are very profound in your remarks, Jafper. Well then, I will agree to fubftitute *Stratford* for *Porto Bello*, and *Avon* for *the Pacific*, though I cannot fay it has deferved that name lately." I then read the Parody, and approved it much; on which Jafper faid, " Will you have any Notes to it?" " No, no, Jafper, it will be underftood plain enough by every failor in that Fleet."

I am, yours truly,
OWEN, Junior.

CAPELL'S GHOST:

To Edmund Malone.

A PARODY.

(The original M. S. is figned W. G—d. with this Motto:

"*In reluctantes Dracones.*"

JASPER HARGRAVE.)

As near honour'd STRATFORD lying,
   Faft by Avon's fwelling Flood,
At midnight with ftreamers flying,
   SHAKESPEARE's gallant Navy rode;
There while EDMUND fate all glorious
   From falfe IRELAND's late defeat,
And the critic crews victorious
   Drank fuccefs to every fheet:

On a fudden ftrangely founding,
   Dubious *notes* and yells were heard,
Grammar, fenfe, and points confounding,
   A fad troop of *Clerks* appear'd;
All in fpotted night-gowns fhrowded,
   Which in life for coats they wore,
And with looks by reading clouded,
   Frown'd on the reviewing fhore.

On them gleam'd the Moon's wan luftre,
   When the fhade of CAPELL bold
His black bands was feen to mufter,
   Rifing from their cafes old.

O'er the glimmering stream he hied him,
    Where THE STEEVENS* rear'd her sail,
With three hundred *Clerks* beside him,
    And in groans did EDMUND hail:

" Heed, oh heed my fatal story,
    I am CAPELL'S injur'd Ghost!
You who now have purchas'd glory,
    Near the place where I was lost.
Though in CHALMERS' *leaden* ruin
    You now triumph free from fears,
When you think of *my* undoing,
    You *must* mix your joy with tears.

Mark the forms by WILLIAM painted,
    Ghastly o'er the harrowing scene,
Envy wan with colours tainted,
    And Detraction's skulking mien.
Mark the passions foul and horrid,
    Low'ring o'er the blasted *Heath*;
Hecate hides her Son's black forehead
    At the scoundrel tale beneath.

I, by Learning's train attended,
    Treasures hid *first* brought to light;
And from none *my* stores defended,
    Who for Shakespeare burn'd to fight,
Oh, that from such friends' caresses
    I had turn'd me with disdain,
Nor had felt the keen distresses,
    Stung by all that serpent train.

                                    Rival

* The Admiral's Ship.

Rival Scholars I ne'er dreaded,
  But in twenty years had done,
What thou EDMUND, little heeded,
  Haſt atchiev'd in two alone.
Then the ſhelves of Cadell never
  Had my foul diſhonour ſeen;
Nor Contempt the ſad receiver
  Of my SHAKSPEARE'S SCHOOL had been.

Warburton and Pope diſmaying,
  And their blunders bringing home,
Though condemn'd to Satire's flaying,
  I had met a Tibbald's doom;
To have fallen, Sam Johnſon crying,
  He has played a Scholar's part;
Had been better far than dying,
  Struck by cowards to the heart.

Unrepining at *ſuch* glory,
  Thy ſucceſsful toil I hail;
Men will feel my cruel ſtory,
  And let CAPELL'S wrongs prevail.
Doom'd in Slander's clime to languiſh,
  Days and nights confum'd in vain,
Worn by treachery and anguiſh,
  Not in open battle ſlain.

Hence with all my *Clerks* attending,
  From their parchment tombs below,
Through their office-duſt aſcending,
  Here I feed my conſtant woe;

                        Here

Here the Commentators viewing,
    I recall *my* fhameful doom,
And my primal notes renewing,
    Wander through the letter'd gloom.

O'er MY SCHOOL for ever mourning,
    Shall I roam deprived of reft,
If to Avon's banks returning,
    You neglect my juft requeft;
After your *dull* foe fubduing,
    When your Stratford friends you fee,
Think on Vengeance for *my* ruin,
    And for SHAKESPEARE fham'd in me!"

(A true Copy from the original M.S. preferved in Mr. OWEN JUNIOR's Chambers, Paper Buildings, Inner Temple:

  (L. S.)   JASPER HARGRAVE,
          Clerk to Mr. Owen, Junior.)

No. VII.

To the EDITOR of the MORNING CHRONICLE,

SIR, *Inner Temple, Oct. 18. 1799.*

OUR correspondence has been a little interrupted by the absence of my friend Jasper, who is but just returned from Bath, where he went on some private business, or amusement. He asked my permission to go, and as he had been so diligent, and given me a proof of his taste, by selecting the Parody called " CAPELL's GHOST, by W. G." I readily indulged him, though of all things Literature will the least admit of any interruption. The habit is gone or relaxed, and it is sometimes resumed with

with difficulty, as every student knows. *Leaden* GEORGE, indeed never tried; he is perpetually " plodding and plodding his weary way," like the ploughman of the poet, though he never gets *home*; and in moſt of his reſearches, " *leaves the world to darkneſs*" in his *droning* flight, and *drowſy* tinklings over Shakſpeare and all his commentators. I wiſh to heaven they were all laid in the Red Sea, with Buonaparte and his hoſt. I know you love Similes, Mr. Editor.

Leaden George " artfully* endeavours (like Shakſpeare againſt Spenſer) to raiſe himſelf on a level with his opponents," Steevens and Malone; and if Shakſpeare were alive, would fain perſuade him,

" There lives more life in one of *his* fair eyes
Than both thoſe Critics can in praiſe deviſe†.

Though upon my word, as a Commentator he is himſelf, what I leave to him and the Britiſh Critic to ſettle between them, a literary *Hermaphrodite*‡. Jaſper, in great ſurpriſe, exclaimed, " What can that be, Sir? but I think I recollect; you allude to one of GEORGE'S *proofs*."—" Juſt ſo, Jaſper, and right pleaſant it is. You remember the great controverſy about Shakſpeare's Sonnets. We are told that there are exactly 154 of them numerically ſtated; 120 of which were addreſſed to a man, and the *remaining* 28 were addreſſed to a lady. Now by George's *calculation*, the two ſums together make only 148, and as there are 154 actually exiſting Sonnets,

---

* Chalmers's Supplemental Apology, p. 40.
† Shakeſpeare, Sonnet 83.
‡ Supplemental Apology, p. 45.

Sonnets, he has *proved* ' by his little skill in arithmetic,' that *six* remain unaccounted for, and *therefore* this balance of six, being addressed neither to man, woman, nor boy, must necessarily be addressed to *an Hermaphrodite*: which was to be *proved*."—" How that will please Professor Mac Taggart, my tutor in the *Humainities*, when I tell him of this *proof* by his countryman!" said Jasper, in an extasy of arithmetical joy, which none but a Cocker or a Chalmers could feel. " I dare say this occasioned much amusement, Sir, among the Clerks of the Council Office."—" Who told you of that, Jasper? You are a wizard; it was actually the case. I know the man who had the very anecdote from Sir Stephen himself about this literary *Hermaphrodite*."—" Pray," said Jasper, " was there a sage Jury impannelled on the occasion, and *an inspection prayed?*" " You are very arch, Jasper; Sir Stephen did not mention that; but it was seriously proposed to have a *leaden* cast of GEORGE CHALMERS set up in the Council Office in that character. Secretary Fawkener and Chief Justice Reeves burst out in a fit of laughter, in a merry conceit how it was possible that any image compounded of *Mercury and Venus*§ could have any resemblance to their old friend George.

" Secretary Fawkner, who is a most excellent Classic, ran over all the passages in Homer and Horace, about the grandson of Atlas, much to the entertainment of Lord Liverpool; but I was very much surprised that he left *Venus* to the illustration of the Lord Chief Justice of Newfoundland, for which I suppose he had his reasons. George who, like Shakspeare, ' kens small Latin, and

---

§ Hermaphrodite, i.e. Hermes and Aphrodite, or Venus.

and no Greek,' thought they were talking about the old statues of the *Hermathenæ*‖, and had no objection to the compliment. You must know, that George conceives himself descended from Minerva and Vulcan by a sort of *left-handed* marriage, from which, as it has happened at *other* Courts, neither the Father, nor *the Mother*, nor the dear offspring, could ever be *introduced at the Court* of Apollo. So, like some other folks, they made *a Court and Theatre of their own*, and put a large *black Eagle* in front of it."

While George was indulging this deep meditation in English, Greek and Latin quotations from Fawkener and Reeves flew about the Council Office as thick as corn on a threshing floor, and puzzled " *the Defender of the Faith,*" as Mr. Ireland always calls him.

" Mais GEORGE, comme le Pere au grand cordon,
Prend son Grimoire, evoquant le Demon,
Le pesant Diable, aux aîles du plomb,
Morphée en Angleterre, et son très cher Patron."

You may imagine there was an end of the dispute, for George, in other words, took out his Supplemental Apology, and read them ten or twelve lines in continuation, and so Lord Liverpool could get no more business done that day at the office. It was all " *quiet good sense* ;" for Secretary Fawkener, Lord Chief Justice Reeves, and all the Clerks felt the *vapeur soporifique du Cordelier Pere Grisbourdon, et son livre de cabale.*

It is said that Mr. Pitt intends to move that his friend George, or le Pere Roc Grisbourdon, should be present when Sheridan and Tierney begin to discuss a late expedition

---

‖ *Hermathenæ.* or Mercury and Minerva.

tion after the adjournment; and when the Minister himself has sufficiently parodied Homer's account of " *the Ships of the Bœotians.*" THE LEADEN MACE will descend with great effect, and save the Speaker infinite trouble. No necessity for calling to *order*, when *Grisbourdon*'s spirit is extended over *all* the Members. Nothing but chromatic semitones, Dutch, French, or English, all equally intelligible, in one drowsy yawn. When I was telling this to JASPER, the dog, who has always something to the point as far as he has read, said, " Yes, Mr. Owen, George will be of infinite use to Pitt on that occasion, and ' make one mighty Dunciad' of the three Estates.

—————————" Who keeps awake?
The Parliament will gape, but cannot speak;
Lost is the Nation's sense, nor can be found,
While *his* long solemn unison goes round:
Wide and more wide it spreads o'er all the realm;
See PALINURUS nodding at the helm;
See Vapours mild o'er each Committee creep,
Unfinish'd Treaties in each Office sleep;
While chiefless armies doze out the campaign,
And Navies *yawn* for orders on the Main."

" Never, never, Jasper;" I replied in haste:—" that will not, cannot be! But I know your patriotic heart spoke this only to be contradicted." " *Audi alteram partem*, is a good maxim," said Jasper, " as Professor Mac Taggart allows: let me hear what you have to offer." " True Jasper, you love a little *Cart and Tierce*; but our friend Brinsley could tell you that ' one thrust in *Tierce* may be fatal, even from a base Beef-eater.' No, no, Jasper:— the Nation's sense is not lost; it is declared and active;

its

it's voice is indeed in folemn *unifon*, and heard loudly and diftinctly in every town and city, in every port, in every village, in every fhip and in every veffel from the Thunderer to the fifhing-fmack. It has declared, England will never fubmit to France, nor her inftruments; fhe will be free while the hearts, and hands, and purfes of her Soldiers, Sailors, Statefmen, and Volunteers can keep her fo. What Jafper? can the Britifh Navy ever faint or fleep, when St. Vincent, Duncan, Nelfon, and Mitchell direct her prows, and deal out her thunderbolts over the Deep? When there is fcarce a promontory, or a cape, or a harbour in the globe, but has felt the force of her arms defenfive, victorious, or coercive? Is not every hoftile Fleet captured, difabled, or blockaded? When the Nations feek for our protection, and court our alliance; when they acknowledge that all which is left of true vigour, fpirit, juftice, and wifdom is connected with Great Britain, her councils, and her arms? Call you this ' *the yawning of our Navies for orders?*' Thefe glories are independent of our divifions about Minifterial perfonalities; thefe are national. What, Jafper!—When we look around us, and fee the gallant ROYAL BROTHERHOOD, not wafting their prime in floth, but alert and in energy for their Country? When you read the names of York, Abercromby, Grey, Harris, Dundas, Moore, and all our brave Commanders, will you call our *Armies Chieflefs?* Learn to know the language and the power of Great Britain: you are no Jacobin, I hope? Look to Ruffia: look to Germany: are the *Treaties unfinifhed?* Look to either India; fee Ifland added to Ifland, and Colony to Colony! Behold the Tyrant of Myfore proftrate, and his death made the feal of Conqueft and of Peace! Is not the Capital of the Eaft our own? Is not the whole Fleet of Belgium in our own

ports

ports?" "Yes, Sir; but not our own Armies in their own Country*," cried Jasper. "Hold, hold," I answered: "we have deserved success, my friend: more gallantry, courage, conduct, or prowess were never displayed than by the Army of Great Britain and her Allies. I wave the private principle of foreign Cabinets; but I feel that OUR COUNTRY *has no cause for dejection in her brave but unfortunate exertions* to obtain Liberty and Property for the miserable and the oppressed. Our Commanders, Sailors, Soldiers, and Volunteers by sea and land have played, all and every of them, an English part; and the character and the dignity of OUR COUNTRY are exalted yet higher by the very obstacles which have been opposed." "Pray, stop, Sir," said Jasper:—" I own I was wrong: I will talk no more of *nodding*, till leaden George comes across me again.

" As I was looking in the chest early this morning I found a kind of Ode, or something like one, just sent to Paper Buildings during my absence at Bath, and the unexpected turn which our conversation, or rather *your rapture*, Mr. Owen, has taken, puts me in mind of it. The Author has not sent a very correct copy, but, if I can make it out, I will put it in my fair round text which you admire so much. It is not foreign to our labours; *lead* and bullets are quite in our way." " Jasper, you are a Wag. Well, I'll call to-morrow and look at it; if I like it, you shall copy it. But, remember you made the last choice; it is my turn now. I must step over to the King's Bench Walks, for I have a Client waiting. I hope you do not want to make any more journies; for I cannot spare you."

At this we parted, though Jasper wished me to give him a furlough from Parnassus for another week or two.

What!

October 13, 1799.

"What!—a Soldier from his post? For shame, Jasper: at a time like this it cannot be. Can't you be contented? You have the best of the business; all the Wits come to you, and you go to none of them, and wait for none of them:

>But we, in Chambers dull,
>Lawyers, like Sentries, are condemn'd to sit
>*From seven to ten,* and waste our brief-less hours,
>Cursing the Attorneys."

I am yours, most truly,

OWEN, Junior.

No. VIII.

To the *EDITOR* of the *MORNING CHRONICLE.*

SIR,   *Inner Temple, Oct.* 29. 1799.

I Was not able to keep my promise with Jasper till this morning, when I called upon him and found him with some French Verses which his Preceptor, the Abbé, had put into his hands. " What, can you read French verse, Jasper; or are you so affected as to think there is no *Poetry* in that language? If you are, take care you don't prove your absolute ignorance of it; and like many *classical scholars*, by reading the verses aloud, shew that you do not understand even the common cæsura, and laws of the metre."—" No, faith," said Jasper, " I never pretend to knowledge where I am ignorant, nor affect contempt where I am deficient in taste. I am as yet only looking at a lesson against the Abbé calls, as I would study an Ode of Horace to profit from the lectures of Professor Mac Taggart, when we read it together." " I wish every body would be as honest, my diligent friend; I'll talk with you hereafter on that subject; at present I

wish

wish to know what you are reading."—" Only a Recueil, Sir, or Book of French extracts; I cannot say from what authors all of them are taken: you see it is a small thin duodecimo, light and easy; not like the ponderous, clumsy, ELEGANT EXTRACTS with which we are pestered here, and children are teazed with at our *Seminaries*, like Manual Lexicons in thick quarto, too heavy to hold in the hand." " You are right, Jasper; the booksellers and their compilers are strangely stupid and unaccommodating in this *Extract-work*. They are not so considerate even as old GEORGE with his *Sugar of Lead:* they think all is cream which swims at the top of any mixture." " City-taste, Mr. Sterling."—" Why, Sir, that is rather an ungracious remark from you, who are employing me in the *Extract*-line, though to be sure there is some difference between a feuille-volante and a volume of a thousand pages, with double columns and in small print, *pour délasser l'esprit*.

" But I cannot tell how it is, I replied, the French will always excel us in that way; they never can be depressed. I am certain you could never sink a literary French Abbé, except you were to tie George's Supplemental Apology on his breast, and send him to rhime in the river, as the Duc de Montausier proposed to do with the Satirists. You might as well think of drowning a cork."
" I suppose," said Jasper, " you know that Leaden George is now in alt; for as his favourite and truly harmonious Satirist, Marston, most poetically sings,

" E'en GEORGE himself now revels with neat jumps:
A worthy Poet hath put on his pumps†.

" Where do you get these uncouth and *pithy* verses, Jasper?" " From George's lumber-house, to be sure, Sir;

---

† Supplemental Apology, Page 230.

Sir; it is all the *poetry* he knows." " 'Faith then I hope George will continue to walk or dance in his new pumps. It fhould be only faid, ' Forth from his office *walks* THE MAN OF LEAD ;' for I hope he never rides on *horfe-back*, as I am fure there is not a charger in his Majefty's Mews equal to his weight."

" But Jafper, what are thefe French lines ?"—" Something, Sir, very flattering to the Londoners, in the expreffion at leaft; a kind of advice or exhortation to writers here, which I fhould think fome of my correfpondents, whofe works are in the Cheft, have read with effect. I do not pretend to pronounce them right as yet; I wifh the Abbé were here to read them himfelf; but there is more in the compliment than the verfe in this cafe." " Let me fee them, Jafper. Well, I perceive the Abbé knows how to flatter and laugh in his fleeve at us, like all his tribe, and can " weigh Port and Partridge againft empty praife." It is pleafant to fee what fools thefe French Abbés make of us every day, even at our own tables."

" Travaille bien, cours en vers t'efcrimer ;
Je veux que LONDRES ait a jamais l'empire
Dans les deux arts, DE BIEN FAIRE ET BIEN DIRE."

" Bravo, Monfieur Abbé !" faid Jafper, " you may have your laugh, and we will verify your words."

" You remember, Sir (if you have not quite forgot every thing in your rapture at the laft vifit you paid me), I told you that I could feel for my Country as well as you, and for every thing compofed either in its honour or vindication, when neceffary. There are few perfons
who

who have read your eloquence on the late well-planned but unfortunate Expedition, without revering with gratitude the valour and conduct of every Commander, Soldier, Sailor, and Volunteer in it. The principle was good: to crush, if possible, the Tyrant and the Oppressor, and to restore Liberty and Property to the captive and plundered Hollanders. I could talk as if our Guardian Deity and Inspirer were present. The Meditation of Theocles in 'The Moralists' would not be more interesting. To be sure, Mr. Owen, a Lawyer in the Temple has in general no prospects, brooks, or groves, no precipices or cataracts to inspire him: if you except Fig tree Court, and the King's Bench Lawn, and the *many-twinkling* feet of Laundresses and Attornies, he has nothing before him but the '*bottomless Pitt*,' which, however, is one source of the Sublime, as Arbuthnot and Burke have *proved*. But if you are fond of Poetry, when the subject is your own Country, here is a kind of FUNERAL ODE, which I mentioned to you; and I know your studies and taste too well to think you will reject it. I shewed it yesterday to a young Barrister of great promise and various talents, who is well versed in the ancient Lyrics, and still reads Pindar, Horace, and Gray, though he has left Christ Church. As he was perusing it, a man of eminence, as a Painter and a Musician, came in, and they both read it aloud with spirit and feeling. I know you would have been pleased, Mr. Owen, if you had been present. They both agreed that it was peculiarly adapted for Music; and the gentleman of the long robe wished that those great harmonists BOYCE and COOKE were alive. I would have put it, said he, into either of their hands. If you think so, said the painter, I know a young, but profound

found compofer in the art, on whom the mantle of thofe great mafters feems to have fallen and refted. The young Barrifter took up the word with eagernefs, and cried out, you mean CALCOTT. I do, faid the painter; and if you fhould perfuade Mr. Owen to permit you to felect this Ode from your cheft for publication, I wifh it may attract the notice of that learned and diftinguifhed young man, who does fo much honour to his profeffion." " You talk this well, Jafper, faid I, but to the proof: the fubject is at my heart, I wifh the words may anfwer to my feelings."—" Sir, faid Jafper, here is a Greek motto, of which I know nothing; the writer fays, it is from one of the Olympics of Pindar: I wifh you would conftrue it to me." " I will, if I can, Jafper; but you may be fure I fhall not print Greek in a newfpaper." I then took the Ode, and you may imagine my opinion, as I confented to fubmit it to your tafte and judgment. " But pray, faid Jafper, what is the meaning of the Greek? Don't go without telling me."—" It is, I replied, as follows briefly, but inadequately; ' Toil, Labour, and Expence always go hand in hand, and fight together with Virtue and Valour, in every enterprize of moment and danger."—" It is to the point, faid Jafper; fuccefs is not the meafure of what is right and juft: the motto, however, may as well be left out. But now for the lyric Mufe. *Favete linguis*, is the old exordium, and it is ftill in force.

I am your's truly,

OWEN, JUNIOR.

THE DIRGE OF BELGIUM.

OCTOBER, 1799.

AN ODE.

HEARD you the ſtrain from yonder Sky
On Albion burſt in choral Majeſty?
　See his throne great Ocean leave;
　　The Deities, who round him wait,
　　Attendant on his State;
　The firm Earth ſhakes; the Billows heave;
And from the deep Tritonian Shell
Slow ſolemn-breathing Notes o'er Belgium pauſe and ſwell!

From

From thy awful rock ferene,
  Holy Freedom, hear and bend;
Thine the heroes, thine the fcene,
  Thine the caufe; great Pow'r, defcend:
On raven plumes, involving all,
Brooding Death unfolds the pall!

'Tis not Superftition's groan,
Frantic yell, or fullen moan,
Philip's gloom and Alva's frown.
Call thy righteous vengeance down;
Godlefs monfters ftalk around:
Hear, and guard this fated ground.

Lo, beyond the Eaftern gate,
Britain bold confirms thy ftate;
By Aurora's earlieft beam,
By the proud and myftic ftream,
O'er the proftrate Tyrant's fway
India hails thy opening day.

See, arous'd in Virtue's caufe,
Sacred Rights and equal Laws,
Armed Nations raise the prayer;
Bid the avenging Eagle bear
Thy thunders from the realms of Paul:
Rife, and crufh the monfter Gaul!

By Andrafte's radiant throne;
By the fphere and wizard ftone;
By old Mador's Druid lyre,
Struck with more than Grecian fire;
Thy words of potency infufe,
Breathing o'er the Patriot Mufe.

Ling'ring on the Belgian shore,
Hallow'd tears see Albion pour
O'er the grave where warriors sleep,
Victors of the subject deep;
There Honour, Virtue, Justice mourn,
Clasping sad their rostral urn.

Holy Goddess, hear and spare;
  Give thy chosen Heroes rest:
Though steep'd in crimson streams of war,
  Soon be the sword in olive drest.
Valour triumphs :—yet they die!
Lift the recording tablet high,
And hail the champion sons of Truth and Liberty.

No.

No. IX.

To the EDITOR *of the* MORNING CHRONICLE.

SIR, *Inner Temple, Nov.* 9, 1799.

My friend and clerk Mr. JASPER HARGRAVE gave me yesterday the Letter which I enclose; and he informed me it was sent to Paper Buildings the day before. As it appears to me of a very strong and serious cast, and founded on just conceptions of the subject, I shall not delay it; and if I am not greatly mistaken, it will correspond to your feelings, Mr. Editor, and to those of every Gentleman in this generous and enlightened Kingdom.

I am yours most truly,

OWEN, Junior.

A LETTER

TO

GEORGE CHALMERS, *Esq. F.R.S.S.A.* AUTHOR OF AN APOLOGY FOR THE BELIEVERS IN THE SHAKE-SPEARE PAPERS.

ON THE SPIRIT AND PRINCIPLE OF THE POSTSCRIPT TO THAT APOLOGY.

SIR, *Wimpole-ſtreet, October* 30, 1799.

I HAVE read what you have publiſhed about the pretended Shakeſpeare Papers, not without receiving ſome little information on the ſubject. It is immaterial to me whether you write in a lively or a heavy manner: on this head indeed you have heard much, and it appears as if you would hear a great deal more. I have peruſed what has been given to the Public in Proſe and Verſe; and I conceive that you will be delivered down to poſterity like the Dennis of Pope, or the Cotin of Boileau. You ſeem to be one of thoſe " Book-wights (deſcribed by a lively modern Writer*) who have miſtaken the drudgery of their eyes for parts and abilities, and have ſuppoſed it beſtowed wit, while it only ſwelled their arrogance and unchained their ill-nature." What you have ſaid to Mr Steevens and Mr. Malone may be well enough in a few particulars, and you have pointed out ſome of their miſtakes.
You

---

* Lord Orford.

You have told the world in your Dedication to Mr. Steevens, that You " are a good fort of man; have writ-
" ten able tracts upon Trade, an elaborate Book of Political
" Annals: have compofed feveral Lives with knowledge
" and elegance; and in all YOUR writings YOU certainly
" give us fomething new, NEW FACTS AND NEW PRIN-
" CIPLES!"——A very modeft eulogium from a man's own pen! and, if fo accurate a judge as Mr. Steevens admits ALL THIS, I fhould think his denial of your knowledge of Shakefpeare can hardly be efteemed a drawback; and it is without juftice that you have changed the learned Editor of Shakefpeare into a Hampftead Apothecary. You tell us that you have no fear of Mr. Steevens's *Cantharides*, and declare yourfelf fully equal to all your labours; though a high Officer of ftate, of your own Country, once candidly confeffed his inability in the Houfe of Commons in this general way.

But I fhall wave the difcuffion of your ability and difcoveries: what I object to is THE PRINCIPLE of your *Poftfcript*, to which I object indeed in a moft folemn way. I write this as one who feel for every perfon who ranks in life as a Gentleman, and has endeavoured to cultivate his talents and communicate his opinions to the public. In your POSTSCRIPT, Sir, you attack a Gentleman *by name* in an outrageous and brutal manner, upon the *mere fuppofition* of his being the Author of an anonymous Poem. You have not proved an iota of your affertion in the fair eftimation of any man acquainted with the nature of proof. You evidently write under the influence of paffion and refentment at fome reflexions caft upon *you* as an Author, and on *your* Book as a compofition. You argue thus—

Becaufe

Because a Gentleman enquires if a Book sells, and if it has a good character, and speaks handsomely of it himself, *he is the publisher of it*; and if the Publisher, then he is *probably* the Author; and then you run on about the doctrine of *probability*, and tell us from a variety of Authors that we must be guided by it in all cases. In a great many cases we certainly must, but not in *such* cases as those you think proper to decide dogmatically. You are like the old Monkish Writers, who, as it is said, could never see a sun-beam break into their cell without being ready to cry out " Fire!"

If this is your method of establishing *facts* upon argument and proof, *your credibility* as a Writer is shaken to its foundation; and the public will naturally be cautious how they put any confidence in your *political* researches and deductions. A ministry must be weak indeed to entrust any investigation to *your* reasoning powers; or who would not blush to consider you among the auxiliary bands of Government. You will be degraded from the rank of a man of information, and consigned to dreams and reveries with Crusoe and his man Friday, in the island of De Foe. It may also be presumed when your *Novels* are collected they will be preserved with Queen Elizabeth's Letters to Shakespeare, and Mrs. Robinson's Memoirs of the *Leaden*-head Family.

I appeal to any Gentleman in this kingdom whether a mere downright assertion on your part, added to what you are pleased to call probability raised upon some doubtful circumstances, is sufficient to authorize you to act offensively, as upon an affirmed and acknowledged proof, when you dare to stigmatize so shamefully a gentleman of some character

in

in the world in the manner you have done, after having made yourſelf WITNESS AND JUDGE in the cauſe. Is it fitting, Sir? Is it decent, is it juſt, is it creditable to yourſelf to call openly upon this gentleman *by name* in the moſt direct and opprobrious language? To affix a work to him which neither he nor any other man ever acknowledged as his writing, and to brand him as a man *impertinent, nonſenſical, malignant, ignorant, abſolutely unable to write proſe or verſe or even to write at all*, and point him out as " *a Jacobin*," a name which, in the preſent acceptation of the term comprehends every thing which is an object of averſion and horror in a civilized nation? I never yet read a book written in *ſuch* a ſpirit, and upon *ſuch* a principle as this Poſtſcript. You ſeem deſirous and eager, if it were in your power, to deprive this gentleman of every particle of good character, and the comforts of exiſtence; to alienate his friends and acquaintance from him, and to *hunt* him from ſociety; and you thirſt to complete his deſtruction with fierceneſs combined with impotence; and all this, *becauſe* YOU, Mr. GEORGE CHALMERS, have a ſtrong *ſuſpicion* that he wrote " The Purſuits of Literature," put a *leaden* Mace in your hand, and termed *you* a ponderous writer, or ſomething to that effect; and this you aſſert without one proof whatſoever, but from conjecture alone.

You ſtile yourſelf " an offenceleſs maſtiff, repoſing in the ſhade after a ſucceſsful conflict†." I know nothing of you in this character; nor can I tell whether it is abſolutely neceſſary for my Lord of Liverpool to keep any gaunt maſtiff, ſuch as you deſcribe yourſelf, to growl

at

† Poſtſcript to Mr. Chalmers's Supplemental Apology, page 496.

at the gate of the Council Office, or frighten beggars from the Board of Trade. It is plain you wish to avenge a personal offence against yourself, committed in eight or ten lines, and you therefore have given the public a ponderous Postcript of one hundred and fifty-nine pages in octavo. It is GEORGE CHALMERS, not our gracious and beloved Sovereign King GEORGE the Third, and the cause of constitutional liberty, which prompts your pen; it is not zeal for THAT GREAT HOUSE *which eats you up*, but private revenge, as an Author, which preys upon you. If your *leaden* Mace had been changed into *gold* by the Writer of the Pursuits of Literature, your studies on trade had been uninterrupted, and the mastiff would have slept on.

But Sir, if you could *prove* your point, which appears to be absolutely impossible after all the attempts which have been made by you and others, you are still to be reprobated for your manner. If you have asserted many things which have no foundation in truth whatever, as I believe, you are wholly without excuse. I care for nothing, however, but the PRINCIPLE of your Postscript; it is meant to strike at every public opinion which is given to the world without a name, and it would destroy every liberty and right of which we are *yet* in full possession. I think too highly of any man of literary eminence, or of any person in power, to conceive that any one of them could employ you to write this shameful and shocking Postscript, or any part of it. I believe it was done of your own mere motion; and from what you have written

ten it muft be evident to the Public, that you have neither candour to fuppofe good meanings, nor tafte to diftinguifh true ones.

Unhappy man! to whom will you fly for defence or palliation of your grofs offences? If you look to that Board to which you have the honour to belong, you will not find an admirer or a vindicator in the diftinguifhed Nobleman who prefides over it: he is too fagacious and converfant in good writing and argument to approve fuch a violation of decency, reafoning, and good manners. If you look round among your colleagues in office, you may read their opinion in the polite filence they maintain on the fubject of your Book: moft of them are men of erudition and fhrewdnefs, and all of them refpect the honour and character of a Gentleman. But, Sir, you will not pafs without notice. The family of Sir Archy Mac Sarcafm will never be extinct. You will ftill have your little levees at the Council Office, and your puny flatterers from beyond the Atlantic; though fuffering Loyalty will fometimes get the better of judgment. The minor glories of Caledonia alfo will diffufe a radiance round you on the mountains of mift. Think not, however, that you are of confequence, becaufe you are noticed. *Coriat* was not without his farcaftic admirers; and your refearches in old books have acquainted you, that no lefs than fixty fonnets of adulation were prefixed to his *Crudities*.

I care exactly as much who the author of the Purfuits of Literature is as I do who are the authors of Junius, and the Heroic Epiftle to Sir William Chambers. I fhould like to know them all, but I have never been convinced by any arguments or probable conjectures I have feen; and I think that your work has clouded the fubject, and placed it in much greater real obscurity than it was before: but that is only a natural consequence of your taking it up. Nay, such is the spirit of your work, that I protest if you were to present the Supplemental Apology and *Postscript* to any learned Society in this country, and the members of it should return you their thanks for the gift, I should conceive that such a Society would shortly after vote their thanks to Peter Pindar Esquire, if he should also think proper to insult them by a present of his valuable writings.

THE PRINCIPLE of your Postscript, I maintain in the face of the whole Kingdom, is pernicious to society; it is inadmissible by philosophers and scholars, injurious in private life, abhorred and rejected by all gentlemen, and unworthy of *this* country to bear, till it loses the spirit which it has always hitherto maintained. You are not an illiterate author; but you are not a bright writer, and you are a bad and inconclusive reasoner. You never invite or entice your readers by sprightliness of imagery or brilliancy of expression. Your grammatical assertions are ridiculous and contemptible, and without any authority but—your own. As a commentator, you may rank with the Dutch Minellius; as an antiquary, in dulness with Thomas Hearne; as a politician, in heaviness with Stockdale's Matter-of-Fact Compilers of State Papers; and as a Gentleman, with those who write *such* compositions as your Postscript. If you continue to write as you have lately done, and think to be noticed or respected by men of taste, candour, reasoning, humanity, or learning, you will be mistaken in your account. You will by no means deprive the world of the pleasure of discovering *for themselves* the authors of anonymous works, and depend upon it you will never have

the

the ability of taking from the public an amusement which, Dean Swift says, is not disagreeable either to them or to an Author, that of *being in the dark.*

I am, Sir, &c. &c.

ANTENOR.

(A TRUE COPY. From the Original M. S. preserved in Mr. OWEN, JUNIOR's, Chambers, Paper Buildings, Inner Temple.)

(L.S.)   JASPER HARGRAVE,
Clerk to Mr. OWEN, JUNIOR.)

No. X.

To the EDITOR *of the* MORNING CHRONICLE.

SIR, *Inner Temple, Nov.* 18, 1799.

IN my Letter (No. VIII.) I forgot to say that, on the envelope of the last Poetical Manuscript which Jasper copied for you, entitled " THE DIRGE OF BELGIUM, October, 1799; AN ODE," the initials of the Author's name who sent it, were so blotted that my Clerk could not possibly decypher them. " It is strange," said Jasper peevishly, " that, if a man now-a-days writes any thing worth reading, he will not give his name to the world. It was not so among the ancients, as Professor Mac Taggart, my Tutor in the *Humainities*, has shewn me again and again."

" I am of your opinion, Jasper : but, pray tell me if you have any Poetical Communications in English which you have selected from the Chest, as worth my inspection?" " Yes, Mr. Owen; there are several ; and I have just copied the titles of some of them, if you
wish

wish to look at the List." " With much pleasure, Jasper: but I hope you have given a specimen of the Poetry." " No: I have not yet had time for that," said Jasper: but, if you like the titles, I will endeavour to decypher the hand-writings; for Poets write, if possible, worse than the Physicians, and when they intend *Æther* for their Patients, too often send a preparation of *Opium*. But here are the titles: you see, Sir, Leaden George has suggested many ideas and poems which relate but little to himself." I took the Paper in my hands, of which the following is a transcript.

A LIST OF SOME MANUSCRIPTS,

IN PROSE AND VERSE,

Transmitted by various Authors to Mr. OWEN, JUNIOR, at his Chambers in Paper Buildings, Inner Temple, and preserved under the care of Mr. JASPER HARGRAVE, Clerk to Mr. Owen.

A TRUE COPY. J. H.

MS. No. I.

THE SHADE OF DANIEL RACE, on the Banks of the Thames, late Principal Cashier of the Bank of England; occasioned chiefly, but not wholly, by the intended residence of ABRAHAM NEWLAND in the rural town of
Brentford

Brentford in the month of August, 1799. A Financial Poem, with Notes by a Committee of the Bank Directors; with an offer of THREE MILLIONS OF VERSES, to be composed in the praise of the Right Hon. WILLIAM PITT, First Lord of the Treasury, and Chancellor of the Exchequer; to be contracted for, and severally written and delivered by instalments at the Minister's Mansion in Downing-Street, by Mr. Pye, Mr. Jerningham, Mr. Boscawen, Mr. Puddicombe, Mr. Southey, and all the best *hands* which the Directors can engage in London, Oxford, and Cambridge. The Verses, to the amount of full THREE MILLIONS aforesaid, to be faithfully numbered by Daniel Giles and Benjamin Winthrop, Esquires and Directors of the said Bank; and the syllables, ten in each line, to be accurately counted by Messrs. Holdsworth and Laverick, Clerks of the Specie.

To the Poem will be added some *winged words* by the Reverend Critic Mr. John Horne Tooke, to be composed at his shop at Wimbledon, to point out the beauties of it to Mr. Secretary Wyndham: together with A POSTSCRIPT of solid and well-foddered materials in Prose, by George Chalmers, F. R. S. and A double S. and Knight of the Leaden Mace, to calm the Minister and the Cabinet after their poetical ecstasy. There is a long Note, signed RICHARD NEAVE and JOHN PUGET, to prove how much it will be for the advantage of the Nation, if Mr. PITT will accept of the said THREE MILLIONS OF VERSES, to be so contracted for and written. Avoirdupoise weight, in lieu of THREE MILLIONS *of Pounds Sterling*, on an approaching exigency, for a renewal of their Charter on the Mons Frumentarius and the territory of St. Bartholomew.

The

The Poem itself will be adorned with fine Engravings of various subjects; a BANCA ROTTA in perspective, but, like the Tower of Pisa, the line of *direction* still falls *within the base*; the Pediment of the East India House, a Statue of Lord Mornington, and of the Generals Harris and Baird, the Seamen's Lobby, Europe sitting on a Horse and Asia on a Camel: in the back-ground a view of the City Barge sailing up the Thames, and an alluring representation of ALDERMAN CURTIS dancing a Minuet at the Lord Mayor's Ball, and receiving the compliments of the Turkish Ambassador on the occasion. There will also be engraved a Vignette of the Embarkation and Return of the gallant troops from Holland, well-designed by an eminent Artist, but executed in *Acqua Tinta*. The whole composition will be in Chiaro Oscuro; with a Frontispiece designed by Thomas Raikes, Peter Thellusson, and Beeston Long, Esquires and Directors; and an elegant Tail-piece in Bas Relief by W. Edwards Esquire, the Accomptant General. The Motto to the Poem is this:

" *Oh, for the warning voice of Him, who saw*
The ruin CONTINENTAL MEASURES *draw*,
What time by perjurable Styx he swore,
To waste on them nor Man nor Guinea more!"

PATRIOTISM, *Canto* III.

REMARKS on the Poem, BY MR. JASPER HARGRAVE.

A Bookseller, in Dean Swift's time, said he knew to a tittle what books, poems, or plays would best go off in a *dry year*, and which it would be proper to expose if the weather-glass fell to *much rain*. I wish I knew such a person

person to consult during the present influence of *Aquarius*, as these MSS. are left to my judgment. They are generally even without the initials of a name, but I should not scruple to hint my suspicions of the real Authors, if some of my master Mr. Owen's best clients should wish to be informed *very* privately, *and promise to tell nobody*. Any of the wits in vogue would serve the turn, as at present at the Theatre the *barren-brained* REYNOLDS is as good as Sheridan, though even Brinsley himself is but an imperfect Representative of the yet unequalled Congreve.—But whoever can make men laugh or stare, either at *Management*, or a South American Tragical Pantomime, answers the purpose. Yet it is not so with the Authors who have sent their works to the Chest under my care.

I cannot now enter fully into the merits of "THE SHADE OF DANIEL RACE;" but I like the manner of a Poem which consists of one entire speech, and the notes thrown at the bottom of the page. The treating the National Debt in a poetical way is too great a violation of probability, but the Apostrophe to GEORGE ROSE, Esq. who tells us in his late pamphlet that " *he has brought home with him good and certain hope*," *(a)* is very interesting; and the surprise the Poet expresses at George's knowing a word about Horace is quite electric, and would shake the Treasury Chambers. I shall not communicate that part in downright charity. There is a beautiful allusion in six or eight lines to the directorial art of turning down a Merchant's Bills offered for discount, and breathing on a man's credit in the city *pro tempore*; this I shall also suppress. But some extracts might be made for the advantage of the country; such

as

(*a*) The motto to Mr. Rose's excellent and satisfactory Pamphlet is this; " Spem bonam certamque domum reporto!" May it be verified!

THE BOOKSELLER.

as the animated lines defcribing the effential intereft of a clofe Union of fuch a Corporation, as the Bank, with the Executive Government of the Country. I fhould alfo wifh to extract the tale of Protogenes and Apelles, newly adapted, which Pliny has actually degraded into a trial between two *Dutch* performers; but this true *Englifh* Poet has taken the ftory into his own hands, comprehended the whole force of painting, and flung drawing, colouring, and the doctrine of light and fhade into THE NOBLE CONTENTION. It is a *political* improvement on Prior. I defpair however of copying it accurately; for if I were to miftake or mifplace any words it would be fatal to fuch a finifhed compofition. I think there is fomething in it which reminds me of the drawing of the Roman School united with the colouring of the Venetian.

JASPER HARGRAVE,
Nov. 16, 1799.

M.S. No. II.

Dedicated refpectfully, but without permiffion, to the Gentlemen of New Lloyd's Coffee-houfe.

THE PURSUITS OF UNDER WRITERS! a Satirical Poem, with Notes by various *Writers*, figned John Julius Angerftein, Bogle French, J. M'Taggart, F. St. Barbe, Capel Cure, William Curtis, Thomas Rowcroft, Antonio Van Dam, J. B. Loufaida, J. T. Vaughan, William Bell, J. Stocqueler, old Miers, &c. &c. and a fublime
Apoftrophe

Apoſtrophe to the Gentleman known by the name of THE DOCTOR in Lloyd's Coffee Houſe. In the courſe of the Work are inſerted poetical deſcriptions of Ships inſured, with goods more valuable than *Virgil (b)* aboard, for the iſlands once fortunate, a Policy in heroic verſe, and a dithyrambic deſcant on Bottomry.

There is alſo an affecting Addreſs to the Earl Spencer Firſt Lord of the Admiralty, by SAMUEL DIXON, Common Councilman, on the propriety and uſefulneſs of the Convoy Act; to which is ſubjoined a profound Diſſertation on the Two per Cent Duty, in which it is proved inconteſtably that the Britiſh Merchants are *now* actually in a worſe ſituation than they were, before they made an offer to Government of that very productive Tax, and praying the attention of Miniſters on the ſubject.

In one of the Notes is given a free Paraphraſe of Horace's Ode, " O Navis, referent in mare te *novi* Fluctus," by BILLY BOS of the Stock Exchange, from the Weſt end of the Town, one ſtanza of which finely deſcribes the Iſle of Man Bonds, and the indiſpenſable neceſſity of them; and in another the Poet makes a beautiful tranſition to LORD BRIDPORT on the great propriety and conſequence of eſtabliſhing *detached ſquadrons of Frigates,* particularly for intercepting the ſuccours to Breſt, and of other veſſels for the deliverance of the Engliſh coaſt from French Privateers. The Author is peculiarly animated on this ſubject, and in a fine phrenzy or rapture, declares that he ſees THE DOLLARS lately carried into Plymouth; but like other Poets, deſpairs of *touching the Spaniſh* himſelf.

The

(b) Navis, quæ tibi creditum
Debes *Virgilium!* &c. Hor. L. 1. O. 3.
    THE BOOKSELLER.

The whole concludes with an oblique view of the Bay of Naples and the *Egyptian Spouse*; a direct description of the port of Hamburgh, and the tears of the West India Merchants, fast trickling on the Quay, with Sugars, Cotton, Coffee, Drawbacks, and Warehouses, swimming before their eyes now, in the language of true poetry, *veiled with a momentary suffusion.*—The motto to the Poem is this:

" *When a succefsful Minifter is Chief Juftice, Poets and Hiftorians become a voluntary Jury.—What fhould we think of the reign of George the Third to be calculated two thoufand years hence by Eclipfes?*" HISTORIC DOUBTS.

REMARKS, by Mr. JASPER HARGRAVE.

The title of this Poem is so full and comprehensive, that I need observe little as to the general interest it would excite in this great Commercial Nation. If it were published and studied deeply in the City, I am persuaded the force of it is sufficient to turn all the West India Merchants, Bankers, and Underwriters into actually existing Poets. I do not think that a Broker would *get a line written* on a policy, from Angerstein or Bogle French, down to the youngest writer in the Coffee house, without introducing it with a " *Cum tot fuftineas,*" or, " While you, GREAT SIR, the floating world suftain,
Our Trade insure, and open all the main."

The whole poem is exquisite, and if it were published would furnish matter for Reviews and Magazines for a twelve-month. It would require much time if I were to make proper extracts from this great and original work, in which the unrivalled Poet alternately takes into his own hands the trident of Neptune, the pen of the Underwriter, and the money shovel of the Banker. His transitions are bold, while the unity of the whole composition is preserved;

ferved; his figures are correct and impreffive; his defcriptions are chafte and accurate; and his Mufe fometimes fails with a trade wind, and at others buffets with tempefts in the Channel. The Poet is a kind of *Panoramift*, but he differs in this particular, that the nearer you approach his figures, the more they ftrike you.—*Ad Referendum.*

JASPER HARGRAVE.

MS. No. III.

The————

I was about to proceed, Mr. Editor, with Jafper's Lift, but it was fo long that I was obliged to poftpone it, though his remarks were pleafant, and the names and defcriptions of the works interefting. As I think it will be pleafing to you if I fend you fhortly a continuation of the Lift, I leave off with lefs regret for the prefent. Jafper faid to me, as I went out of the room, "I know it is Term time, and that is a *damn'd* drawback on poetry; but I hope you will find a leifure half hour." "Not fo hafty, my friend: if you *fwear* fo much, I fhall really take you for one of our buffoon players in difguife, who *now* can fcarcely fpeak ten words at Covent Garden or Drury Lane without a " damn it " in their mouths. I wonder fuch excellent and pious men as the Managers

do

do not put a stop to the custom; or if they do not, I hope the audience will do it for them."—" I stand corrected," said Jasper, " and will not enliven my speech in this way for the future." " I believe you," I replied, " and every sensible man, if he thought a moment, would make the same resolution." I then took my leave, and if you, Mr. Editor, approve Jasper's diligence half as much as I do, you will never repent of the attention you have given to the communications, which you have received through my hands.

I am your's, most truly,

Owen, Junior.

No. XI. and No. XII.

To the EDITOR *of the* MORNING CHRONICLE.

SIR,   *Inner Temple, Nov.* 29, 1799.

ON my return to Jasper this morning, he gave me the List of Poems and Fragments, whose titles he had copied, and of which I sent you a specimen in my last Letter. "Mr. Owen," he said, "I am so convinced of your taste, that I have actually copied out the whole of No. III. which I have shewn to Professor Mac Taggart, who was so much pleased, that he wrote a few illustrations on the Poem with his own hand; and I have also given some, wherever I thought they were required." "I hope you have not been prolix, Jasper: but I like to understand a Work fully, if I can." "Not very long, Sir; but you shall see." He then presented me with the following composition.

Original

Original MS. No. III.

THE EDITOR, THE BOOKSELLERS, AND THE CRITIC.

AN ECLOGUE.

THE ARGUMENT.

Mr. IRELAND, *the Editor of the Shakefpeare Papers*, Mr. EGERTON*, *and* Mr. BECKET, *the one a Military, the other a Civil Bookfeller, met at* Mr. STOCKDALE'S *fhop in Piccadilly on the day after the intelligence arrived of the new Revolution in the Government of France, under the* Tri-confular *Power in the perfons of Ducos Sieyes, and Buonaparte*. Mr. CHALMERS *happened to be there at the time, with various Gentlemen who had been the fubject of much public difcuffion and converfation. Mr. Stockdale, who always obferves propriety in whatever he does or propofes to do, was fuddenly feized with a defire that an Arcadian† Converfazione fhould take place between Mr. Ireland, Mr. Egerton, and Mr. Becket; and, having previoufly whifpered his intention to them, moved that a felect party fhould retire for the purpofe into his parlour. The ingenious Editor and the amiable Bookfellers confented on this condition, that Mr. Chalmers fhould take the Chair as Prefident. Mr. Chalmers, with his ufual courtefy, candour, and politenefs fmiled, and feated himfelf.* THE LEADEN MACE *being placed on the Table, he nodded to Mr. Egerton, and Mr. Egerton firft addreffed Mr. Ireland.*

The Illuftrations
By J. MAC TAGGART, *Profeffor of the* Humainities, *from Aberdeen,*
and
Mr. JASPER HARGRAVE, *Clerk to Mr. Owen, Junior.*

---

* Of the Military Library, Whitehall, and one of the St. Martin's Volunteer Corps.
† The reader will find by the refult how much Mr. Stockdale was miftaken in his *Arcadian* ideas.—JASPER HARGRAVE.

THE SPEAKERS IN THE ECLOGUE.

Mr. IRELAND, *the Editor of the Shakespeare Papers.*
Mr. EGERTON, *a Military Bookseller.*
Mr. BECKET, *a Civil Bookseller.*
Mr. CHALMERS, *a Critic and President.*

The SCENE; *Mr. Stockdale's Parlour, in Piccadilly:*
THE TIME; *Monday* Nov. 18. 1799.

MR. EGERTON.

O THOU, by Nature form'd, or happier Art,
To trace the windings of Man's easy heart,
And prove, tho' oft unwelcome beams intrude,
All love delusion, or themselves delude;
Begin, my IRELAND, for 'tis thine to cope
With proud MALONE, and more presumptuous POPE. (a)
See JERNY's (b) "younglings are but just awake,"
And Cuddy PYE the Tritons (c) teaze and shake;

See

(a) It will soon be discovered who has assumed this title.—JASPER HARGRAVE.

(b) It is not easy to determine to which of Mr. Jerningham's "younglings" Mr. Egerton alludes; but it is really astonishing that such a Writer, whose characteristics are *feebleness and inanity*, should think himself qualified to make the greatest Orator of France, BOSSUET, *speak English.*——JASPER HARGRAVE.

(c) See Mr. Laureat Pye's Naval Poem, entitled NAUCRATIA, in which the *Salt Water* has had no effect on his Poetical Constitution, which sadly wants a little bracing.—JASPER HARGRAVE.

See there the tender, simple-minded Swain,
BOSCAWEN ambling (*d*) on the Sabine plain;
FITZGERALD, SOTHEBY, Poets of the Nile,
Provoke the sneer, and make e'en NELSON smile:
Yet what are all their feats, their classic claim,
Their jinglings, jugglings—to thy sovran (*e*) fame,
Where Thames' and Avon's kindred waters meet,
A mingled Current, fast by Norfolk-street?
What time in saffron sock PARR (*f*) bless'd the day,
And WARTON chanted soft the spousal lay;
The Owl of Somerset, the Soland Goose,
And the Bat flitted o'er the auspicious noose;
While Art diffus'd around thy magic room
From Stars of yellow glass a golden gloom,
And bade the entranced visitant survey
Thy pure mosaic, and thy rich inlay,
The dusky parchment, and the nicer stain
Dy'd on the page in Stratford's antique grain:
Hail! and the Rod of SHAKSPEARE wield alone:
See thy own CHALMERS, Champion of thy Throne!

Mr.

(*d*) It is an odd observation of Horace, that "*Offenduntur quibus est* EQUUS." See Boscawen's Translation.—J. HARGRAVE.

(*e*) "*Sovran.*" The word is written in this manner in compliment to Mr. Ireland, who admires unusual and sublime spelling.——J. HARGRAVE.

(*f*) Alluding to the testimonies of the learned and intelligent to the authenticity of the Shakspeare Papers, with all the signatures, too numerous and too well known to transcribe, viz. Dr. Parr, &c. &c.—J. H.

MR. IRELAND.

How sweet, my EGERTON, thy rapt'rous voice!
Clear is thy head, and CHALMERS is thy choice.
'Twas mine to dive in Earth with step profound
For Prosper's Staff, and bid my Plummet sound
The depths, where buried slept his wizard roll,
And Common Truth and Common Sense control;
No giant task, " weak masters as they are,"
Their nerves all pliant, and their semblance fair;
Well sung the Knight, that " Pleasure is as great
Of being cheated deftly, as to cheat."

MR. BECKET *(g)*.

Avaunt!—nor hope from me endearing sounds,
Nor tongue light-tripping o'er these Fairy grounds:
No, miserable Pair!—with scorn I view
Your Scrip Arcadian, and your Stockings Blue.

Have

(g) In this speech the reader will perceive the tremendous effects of ungovernable passion on a poetical mind like Mr. Becket's which, though enthusiastic, is generally led by the softer Muses. There is much of the sublime and terrible graces in his Address to Mr. Egerton, enforced by the boldest figures, not without the cadence and harmony of the elder Bards. Mr. Becket is possessed with the whole soul of Ajax, the appropriated Hero of all deep resentment.

BECKET in arma prior, nulloque sub Indice venit;
Nec refert, verus furor ille an creditus esset!
   J. MAC TAGGART, Professor of the *Humainities*
     in Aberdeen.

Have ye not heard, when o'er the trembling Foe
My loud *Auruncian* Trump on high 'gan blow,
How Sophists, Poetasters, Atheists fled,
And e'en some Ministers would droop the head;
Impostors, Hirelings, Dastards, all stood mute,
Abash'd, confounded in MY *(h)* fam'd PURSUIT?
IRELAND, from thee I turn: thy views are known,
Left to the boards of Drury, and MALONE.
But THOMAS, thou base Bookseller, retire
To CURL, and MIST, or modern DUTTON's Choir:
See DILLY *(i)* frowns, with RICHARD *(k)* by his side;
And NICOLL, of Pall-mall the prop and pride,

Chief

(h) I have it in my power to announce to the Public, without the least doubt or hesitation, that Mr. THOMAS BECKET, Bookseller, in Pall-mall, is the sole and unassisted Author, Composer, and Publisher of " THE PURSUITS OF LITERATURE." He has come forward candidly, and openly confessed it, *like a man*; and I can add also, what is not so generally known, that about a year ago Mr. B. was summoned before the P——y C————l- and severely examined touching his celebrated Poem, by Mr. P. Lord G. Lord L————gh, Mr. D. the M————r of the R————s, the A————y G————l, and other Officers of State; and, though the utility and merit of *his* Work was allowed BY ALL THE MINISTERS, *nem. diss.* yet he was saved from actual commitment by the interference and friendly pleasantry of Lord L————gh alone. But can it be a matter of surprise that ACIS should yield to the blandishments of GALATEA?—From an Anonymous MS. communication, *penes me*, JASPER HARGRAVE.

(i) THIS PROCESSION OF INDIGNANT LONDON BOOKSELLERS with Mr. Dilly at their head frowning, as they pass on their Military Brother Egerton, is finely imagined, and is peculiarly terrific. Whether the idea was taken from the *Seven Chiefs against Thebes* by Æschylus, or the spectres of the Kings in Macbeth by Shakspeare, I cannot determine

Chief of that sprightly Band, whose mirth and peace
Nor can admit, nor yet desire *increase (l)*;
Botanic WHITE rejects thee, solemn PAYNE,
And splendid EDWARDS with Morocco train;
WALTER, on whom Arabian glories smile,
His *Phœnix (ll)* bold o'er Learning's funeral pile;
And CADELL, panting for the Civic Crown, *(m)*
Swords, chains, and giants figur'd on his gown;
And Lydian ROBINSON, whose purse and press
Nor WALPOLE could affright, nor JONES distress; *(mm)*
And RIVINGTON, to whom e'en Bishops bow,
ELMSLEY the shrewd, and dark-brown BREMNER's brow;
He too, whose orb with smiles alternate greet
The Sons of Cam and Nymphs of Oxford-street,
Accommodating LUNN *(n)*, whose rise and fall
VINCE best descries o'er Granta's learned ball.

See

---

termine; but I think Mr. Becket is, like the son of Euphorion, impetuous, abrupt, sublime.—J. MAC TAGGART, Professor of the Humainities.

(*k*) Richard Cumberland, Esq. a great friend of Mr. Dilly and his learned Patella.

"Archaicis conviva recumbere lectis."

J. MAC TAGGART, Professor, &c.

(*l*) Mr. Becket seems to allude to some agreeable Society or *Club*, which is *Unincreaseable*, as it should appear. I despair of the precise meaning of this rather obscure passage.—JASPER HARGRAVE.

(*ll*) A Bookseller auspicious to the rising of Science, at the *Phœnix* Insurance Office.

(*m*) Mr. Alderman CADELL, now in just and eager expectation of

"Pomps without guilt, of bloodless swords and maces,
Glad chains, warm furs, broad banners, and broad faces."
See, to what distinction and dignity Literature conducts it's patrons and votaries! JASPER HARGRAVE.

(*mm*) Horace Walpole's and Sir W. Jones's Works, the one in five volumes, the other in six Volumes, *Imperial Quarto!*

See LACKINGTON, at whom the Mufes ftare,
Bound in their Temple faft by Munroe's-fquare (*nn*);
At thee e'en JOHNSON ftarts, and either BELL,
(One mourns his *Monk*, and one rings *Crufca's* knell),
Repentant RIDGWAY, PHILIPS from the Seine
The Pamphlet Tribes, dull, felfifh, low and vain,
With the ftrange, motley, Gallic, German crew,
Who feaft and ftarve by turns on KOTZEBUE;
All, all difdain thee in this *focial* age!—
But wherefore wafte my Bibliopolifh rage?
Nor Bookfeller art thou, nor Books thy care:
Camps are thy Shops—thyfelf a Man of War!
Hence to yon Guards, where WYNDHAM's palate nice
On *Ceftrian (o) parings* feeds his Clerks, like Mice;

Where

(*n*) W. H. LUNN, of the Claffical, Philological and Mathematical Library, No. 332, Oxford-ftreet, and in Cambridge, who is faid to divide his learned attention between *thefe two* Seminaries, to accommodate all parties. I am told that in the Cambridge Almanac his *rifing* and *fetting* in the Univerfity is accurately calculated by the Rev. S. Vince, the Plumian Profeffor of Aftronomy, in the fame manner with that of *Venus*; when W. H. LUNN will be a *Morning*, and when an *Evening Star*, on which obfervation much depends in that luminous Univerfity.— J. MACTAGGART, Profeffor of the *Humainities*.

(*nn*) Mr. Lackington has very aufpicioufly placed the Temple of the Mufes clofe to Bedlam.—J. H.

(*o*) Ufed in compliment to Mr. Windham's celebrated *Cheefe-parings*; but the Right Honourable Secretary has fince adopted a Sertorian, or rather *Sartorian* phrafeology, and advifed us not " to cabbage from our own coat." *Q.* Metellus an Elliot?—In the Report on THE NATIONAL CHEESE, it appeared that Mr. Lewis, the Deputy Secretary at War, had more than *eighteen thoufand* flices of *a pound fterling each*, to his own fhare, above three times the quantity allowed to THE GREAT MOUSE, or Firft Lord of the Treafury and Chancellor of the Exchequer united; and the other Clerks *Ex* and *In* (*Tray, Blanch,* and

Sweetheart

Where LEWIS smiles at SHERIDAN and Wit,
BURKE and Reform, and Eloquence and PITT;
There plead with trumpet-tongue thy crimson trade,
Tactics and Triggers, Breechings and Brigade;
There mount thy Austrian Cock and Austrian Tail,
And turn the Fencibles of Pindus pale!
Yet boast not thou, vain Renegado Knight,
Thy patriot soul, and ardour in the fight;
Seest thou those mournful Bands, and prudent YORK,
Those Samnite trenches, and that Caudine Fork?
Ah, more than Traitor to thy Country's cause,
Her ill-starr'd prowess, and her injur'd Laws,
Thou friend to BRUNE, and DAENDEL's best Ally;
Hence: and my deep-aim'd, righteous vengeance fly!
By thee BRITANNIA first was taught to crouch:—
If e'er short slumbers ease thy guilty Couch,
Thee, Caitiff, shall Sir RALPH, the Soldiers' Friend,
And gallant MOORE, and hapless MORRIS rend,
And curse with me, with all, that fatal day
When thou couldst empty send Sir RALPH away,
(Thou shame and scorn of Martin's gallant train,
With plumbean Auster heavy on thy brain),
And dare prefer, to patriot feelings cold,
Chalmerian Lead to RALPHO's proffer'd gold *(p)*.

CHALMERS

Sweetheart) all in fair proportion. It is imagined they will never let the Cheese drop from their mouths, except a Vulpine Committee should flatter them into a Song, which is very much to be desired.—J. MACTAGGART, Professor of the Humainities.

(*p*) The entire failure of the Expedition to Holland has been attributed by the best and most candid judges (and not by Mr. Becket alone) to Mr. Egerton's unfortunate refusal of General Sir Ralph Abercrombie's offer, *on the part*

CHALMERS had lock'd the Dutch in senseless sleep,
Nor left DUNDAS and PITT to wake and weep,
Sad Ministry! —yet righteous sure their aim,
Just every plan, and *thine alone* the blame.

Hence: in thy dream may Gallia's Chief ascend,
The Star of JULIUS beaming on his end;
May Harpies rise, and Gorgons fierce Invade,
And the dread form of THE TRICORPORAL SHADE! *(q)*
The God of Sleep abhors thy visage pale;
Nor e'en the Lead of CHALMERS shall avail!

Mr.

---

part of Government, to take the whole impression, *ad valorem*, of Mr. CHALMERS'S SUPPLEMENTAL APOLOGY and POSTSCRIPT *en masse*, to be shipped and used as *sheet-lead* against the French and Dutch. The minute account of this transaction was related in the Chalmeriana, No. III. It was notorious to the whole kingdom that Mr. Chalmers's LEAD would have done ten times the execution that any other species would: but such is the respect in this Country for private property, that the Minister, though repeatedly urged, could not be prevailed on to put it in State Requisition. Hence the failure of the whole Expedition, and hence the indignation of the Poetical Bookseller against his Military brother.—JASPER HARGRAVE.

(q) This phrase and the application of it would be allowed to be happy even by *our own* Campbell, in his "Philosophy of Rhetoric." The new Revolutionary Monster, or, the Provisional Tri-Consular Power in the persons of DUCOS, SIEYES, and BUONAPARTE, with all their Satellites in the plenitude of Military Despotism, cannot be better expressed than in Virgil's words,

Gorgones, Harpyiæque, et FORMA TRICORPORIS UMBRÆ!

J. MAC TAGGART, Professor of the *Humainities* at Aberdeen.

Mr. Egerton. *(a)*

Loud words, good Sir, the sense alone offend;
But Authors shake, when Booksellers contend:
Anger like thine is madness in degree;
This truth from Horace take, or learn of me.
Ah, think of Lintot, think of Cibber's fame,
Who gently took all that ungently came;
In Fuller too this homely proverb see,
" Two of the self-same trade can ne'er agree."
When Chremes-like *(b)* I heard a Brother speak,
I thought, my Becket, thy discourse was Greek!

Thou

(*a*) Mr. Egerton in his reply to Mr. Becket appears to that advantage, which a man who is cool and in possession of himself must necessarily have over one who is transported by any passion or ecstacy. Mr. Egerton's military character, as one of the St. Martin's Volunteer Corps, will account for his calm, collected state of mind. The ease, the softness, and the simplicity of his speech is finely contrasted with the Papinian or Theban violence of Mr. Becket, which nothing but the fervour of Patriotism could excuse in that learned and poetical, but rather hasty, Bookseller. The unaffected display of his Volunteer services in arms, the candid acknowledgment of his fatal error in Politics, and the *amende honourable* which he offers to his Country, must for ever number Mr. Egerton, of the Military Library Whitehall, among the most distinguished friends of Great Britain. *Si non erraſſet, fecerat ille minus,*—J. Mac Taggart, Professor of the *Humainities*, &c.

(*b*) A beautiful allusion to Horace and his Art of Poetry;
—————Interdum vocem *Comedia* tollit;
Iratusque Chremes tumido *delitigat* ore.
For the propriety of these allusions see *our own* Campbell's Philosophy of Rhetoric. J. Mac Taggart, Professor, &c.

Thou know'ſt, I ever as companions choſe
Thy various verſe and many-languag'd proſe; *(c)*
Thine is the Critic's, thine the Poet's wreath,
And down thy Mall Cremona's gales ſhall breathe!
Thou know'ſt, how gentle by the coaly Shore
My Arms, my Lilts, my Faculties I bore;
How in yon Mews I took my fearleſs ſtand,
And cock'd my piece at valiant CRAIG's *(d)* command.
But though, by WYNDHAM's dialectics preſt,
I ſtill denied Sir RALPHO's high requeſt *(e)*,
Think not my heart can Gallic phrenzy feel,
Or I regardleſs of my Country's weal.
No!—then to Engliſh might DUNDAS pretend,
Or PITT receive ONE POET for his friend;

Gout

(c) I have been credibly informed that Mr. Egerton conſtantly places "The Purſuits of Literature," the ſole compoſition of Mr. Becket, under his pillow, to aſſiſt his midnight meditations. A Soldier, like Mr. Egerton, always has the example of Cæſar before his eyes, as Lucan deſcribes him;
    Media inter prœlia ſemper
  Stellarum Cœlique plagis, Superiſque vacavi!
How *neat and appropriate!*—J. MAC TAGGART, Profeſſor of the *Humanities*, &c.

(d) ALEXANDER CRAIG, Eſq. Examining Clerk of the Board of Works, one of the Commanders of the St. Martin's Corps of Volunteers.—JASPER HARGRAVE.

(e) i. e. Mr. Egerton's direct refuſal of General Sir Ralph Abercromby's offer on the part of Government to take the whole of Mr. Chalmers's Supplemental Apology ad valorem, *en maſſe*, to be ſhipped on the late expedition as *ſheet lead*, and uſed againſt the Dutch. See a former Illuſtration.—JASPER HARGRAVE.

Gout yield to Metals, or Magnetic touch;
Or PORTLAND gabble Demarara Dutch (*f*);
Of Worms and Pills Sir ARCHY ceafe to *fing*,
Or CARLISLE echo back the praife of CHING (*g*)!
No!— my ideas, from fenfation fprung
And ftrong reflection (*h*), high my fancy ftrung,

Taught

(*f*) Since the capture of all the Foreign Settlements of the Dutch in Surinam, and Demarara, I am informed that Mr. Pitt, Mr. Dundafs, the Duke of Portland, Lord Grenville, the Earl of Chatham, Lord Chancellor Loughborough, and Mr. Wyndham, have been deeply engaged in ftudying Dutch under Mr. Janfon, Profeffor of Languages to the Duchefs of York, to enable them to fpeak and write it fluently, and in grammatical purity; but Mr. Pitt, as I hear, though of infinite quicknefs of apprehenfion, has made little progrefs in that fafcinating language, and the Cabinet fay, there is but little hope of the Duke of Portland's *proficiency*. Hence Mr. Egerton's calm affertion.—JASPER HARGRAVE.

(*g*) Mr. Egerton refers to a beautiful and affecting Epiftolary Duet, *fung* every other day between Sir Archibald Macdonald, Lord Chief Baron of the Exchequer, and the Hon. and Rev. Dr. Edward Vernon, Lord Bifhop of Carlifle, in honour of Mr. CHING and his WORM PILLS. See every newfpaper in the kingdom. It appears alfo from fome other clear and valuable letters given to the public, that the Vice Chancellor and the Efquire Beadles of the Univerfity of Oxford have been grievoufly troubled with worms, but Mr. CHING has purged that celebrated Univerfity to its found and priftine health; for which he deferves an epiftle in verfe himfelf, and he fhall have one, if I have time to copy it fair.—JASPER HARGRAVE.

(*h*) Mr. Egerton always adopted Mr. Locke's fyftem; and his known fettled diflike and contempt of *Scotch* Metaphyfics have alienated Mr. Chalmers's affection from him, and I think very juftly.—J. MAC TAGGART, Profeffor, &c. from Aberdeen.

Taught me to prize o'er all domestic peace,
And in the germ bid factious Scions cease.
Better, when Sugars fell and Taxes rose,
Merchants and Traders should o'er Income doze;
Better their senses in oblivion steep,
That all, who bear not arms, might sink in sleep;
Better *at home* might drizzling CHALMERS rain
Drops Paregoric on the public brain;
For sure I deem'd, misled by vulgar fame,
Lethéan Lakes and Belgian Dykes the same!
Ah me! too late my Country's woes I mourn:—
Hadst thou, profound APOLOGIST (*i*), been torn
By Patriot Arms from my reluctant side,
Thy Leaves of *Lead*, without thy person, tried;
Helder had still in proud defiance stood,
And Holland felt old England's Walls of Wood;
Stanhope had ne'er, on Albion's sea-girt (*ii*) Place,
With Burdett chuckled o'er our dire disgrace;
No Russ denounc'd our tardy steps to PAUL (*k*);
No BRUNE exclaim'd, " Capitulate, or Fall:"

Pardon

(*i*) This sublime and unexpected transition and apostrophe to Mr. Chalmers may rank among the happiest efforts of poetry in any language. In this manner Virgil,
 Tu, Nubigenas, invicte, bimembres,
Hylæumque Pholumque manu, tu Cressia mactas
Prodigia, &c.
J. MAC TAGGART, Professor, &c.

(*ii*) I suppose Mr. Egerton alludes to Lord Stanhope's and Sir Francis Burdett's *Marine Conferences* in *Albion Place* at Ramsgate, during the embarkation of the troops for Holland in October last.—JASPER HARGRAVE.

(*k*) " Our Allies, from causes unknown to me, *were two hours too late.*" General Hessan's Letter to the Emperor

Pardon this home-felt truth, thou man of weight!—
I bow to YORK, Sir RALPHO, and the State.

MR. CHALMERS.

Ah! thus deform'd can Bookſellers appear,
One pale with rage, and haggard one with fear?
But who ſhall e'er, when wordy ſtorms rage high,
To BECKET or to CAPANEUS (*m*) reply?
What, like DARIUS (*n*) at my utmoſt need,
Muſt I without a friend deſerted bleed?
To thee, thou patron, dæmon (*o*) of my book,
The Scot exclaims, "Where got'ſt thou that (*p*) Gooſe-look?"

No

---

peror Paul. See the Peterſburgh Court Gazette, Oct. 22, 1799. But ſee our own Gazette, and the report of every Britiſh Officer of diſtinction in the moſt direct oppoſition to it.—JASPER HARGRAVE.

(*m*) How terrific is this alluſion to Statius by Mr. Chalmers, now on the verge of diſtraction himſelf!
Bella protervi
Arcados, atque alio CAPANEUS horrore canendus!
J. MAC TAGGART, Profeſſor, &c.

(*n*) The broken, affecting, melancholy interruptions of ſenſe in *the twelve following lines*, occaſioned by the rapid unconnected tranſitions of ideas, in which Mr. Chalmers calls up ſucceſſively Perſians, Greeks, Romans, Scots and Engliſh, Darius, Macbeth, Dolon, Shakſpeare, Mr. Egerton, Julius Cæſar, Lord Bolingbroke, St. Martin, Pope, and Sir Ralph Abercromby, in a mixed congregated confuſion of words, hiſtory, and metaphors, ſtrongly mark the diſturbed ſtate of Mr. Chalmers's imagination, and the phrenzied impotence of that unhappy Critic.
"So fits give vigour, juſt when they deſtroy."
J. MAC TAGGART, Profeſſor, &c.

(*o*) Addreſſing Mr. Egerton. It is difficult to conceive a ſituation more melancholy and diſtreſſing than Mr. Egerton's;

No warrior thou: a low, mean, hireling Spy,
In SHAKSPEARE's camp, like DOLON, sent to pry:
Thee from my vengeful arm, thus basely fold,
Nor MARTIN shall protect, nor RALPHO's gold.
Yet, though too plain these pages (*q*) must pretend
THOU wert my *guide*, my bookseller, and friend,
Think not this wounded spirit e'er shall call,
" THOU TOO, MY EGERTON?"—then CHALMERS fall.

No: to thee, IRELAND, for relief I turn,
For thee and SHAKSPEARE with like ardour burn:
'Tis all vain impotence; to pigmy bulk
MALONE shall shrink, and dastard STEEVENS skulk.
See'st thou this POSTSCRIPT (*r*)? Shall it e'er be said,
" My saws were toothless, and my hatchet *Lead* (*s*)?"

Did

Egerton's; he is totally deprived of the friendship of Mr. Chalmers, and left in full possession of his book.

(*p*) *Goose.* " A large fowl, proverbially noted, I know not why, for foolishness." Dr. Johnson's Definition; Engl. Dict.—JASPER HARGRAVE.

(*q*) i. e. Mr. C.'s Supplemental Apology and Postscript.

(*r*) The Knight of the Leaden Mace himself, and all the readers of *his Postscript*, will in no very long time be forced to accede to the following description and opinion of it:
" Sans rien omettre, il raconta fort bien
" Ce qu'il savoit:—*mais il ne savoit rien.*"
JASPER HARGRAVE.

(*s*) A line from Pope, adopted by Mr. Chalmers, and said to be constantly in his mind.

Did ever Indian with more brutal knife
Scalp; yet preferve the quivering ftrings of life?
Did ever Prieft, in MOLOCH's gloomy fane,
More grimly pleas'd with blood his idol ftain?
Curfe on my ftar! I hear AUGUSTUS cry,
Forbear; MARCELLUS (t) fhall not, cannot die.
To SATURN's orb my dufky flight I'll wing,
And fail incumbent o'er his fullen Ring (u);

BECKET

(t) Marcellus—Mr. THOMAS BECKET, Bookfeller, the fole unaffifted author and publifher of the Purfuits of Literature. But if any man fhould be fo unwarrantably fceptical as even to hint a doubt of Mr. B.'s free, voluntary, and manly confeffion and depofition, there is not, *at prefent*, one iota of evidence againft any other perfon of what rank, name, or diftinction foever.

 WM. OWEN, jun. Barrifter at Law.
 J. MAC TAGGART, Profeffor of the Humainities.
 JASPER HARGRAVE, Clerk to Mr. OWEN, Jun.

(u) THE TRANSIT OF CHALMERS OVER THE PLANET SATURN would make a fine fubject for the pencil of Mr. Fufeli, and might be engraved on a large fcale as a tranfparent print, and placed on the table during the readings of the Society of Antiquaries at Somerfet Place. Though the CHALMERIAN TRANSIT may perhaps be beft feen through a *fmoaked* glafs, yet it is imagined from fome late *penetrating* difcoveries communicated by Dr. Herfchell to the Royal Society, that Mr. Chalmers will be vifible even to the naked eye in his flight, and in his own dimenfions, confiderably beyond the fphere of Mars, and in the confines of Jupiter. But according to the very *intelligible* doctrine of the French Citizen Aftronomer Lambert, namely, that *diftance* does not diminifh the brightnefs of a great luminous object, I am told that Dr. Mafkelyne, the Aftronomer Royal, has given it as his opinion, that Mr. CHALMERS will appear *as bright* when hovering *over the ring of Saturn*, as he does now when viewed from Oxford, Cambridge,

BECKET shall howl beneath, remote from *Jove*,
Nor in the fields of *Mars* that Recreant (*x*) rove;
But each with groans mephitic air shall draw,
Embrac'd by *Scorpion* (*y*) with contracted claw.

HE foam'd and paus'd; then with a blasting look,
THE PONDEROUS SCEPTRE from the table took;
One stroke he aim'd at each devoted Elf,
But felt reflected vengeance on himself;
Saturnian vapours from his *Mace* ascend,
His words, his strength, his wrath in slumbers end:
The Parlour own'd one universal nap.
And STOCKDALE yawn'd, and sunk on CHAUCHARD's Map (*z*).

---

bridge, Greenwich, or Stratford, *over the meridian of London.*—J. MAC TAGGART, Professor, &c.

(*x*) Mr. Egerton.

(*y*) I think this is an improvement on the delicate Mantuan compliment to Augustus concerning the politeness of *Scorpion*, when he offered to make room for the Emperor upstairs. But on my starting this opinion, Mr. Jasper Hargrave was more inclined to consider it as alluding to the fraternal embrace of a modern French Director or Consul, to which, as to a Scorpion, Mr. Chalmers appears eager to consign the two Poets, Becket and Egerton. Perhaps he is right; yet consult Professor Heyne's Excursus on the *Cœli justa pars.*—J. MAC TAGGART, Professor of the Humainities.

(*z*) A celebrated Map of Germany by CAPTAIN CHAUCHARD, now re-printing under a numerous and most respectable patronage, by Mr. STOCKDALE, who hopes that as not a single copy will be touched by Mr. Chalmers or his Leaden Mace previous to it's delivery, no one will sleep over it, but himself.—JASPER HARGRAVE, Nov. 1799.

THE END OF THE ECLOGUE.

P. S.

(P.S.)   SIR,

It is my intention to tranfmit to you fhortly the titles or contents of the remaining part of the Lift, as I doubt not it will be agreeable to you and your readers.

I am Your's, &c. &c.

OWEN, JUNIOR.

To be continued.

Mr. IRELAND's
Vindication of his Conduct,

RESPECTING

THE PUBLICATION

OF THE

Suppoſed Shakſpeare MSS.

BEING

A PREFACE OR INTRODUCTION

TO

A REPLY

TO THE CRITICAL LABORS OF

Mr. MALONE,

IN HIS

" ENQUIRY INTO THE AUTHENTICITY OF
" CERTAIN PAPERS, &c. &c."

LONDON:

PUBLISHED BY MR. FAULDER AND MR. ROBSON, NEW
BOND STREET; MR. EGERTON, WHITEHALL;
AND MESSRS. WHITE, FLEET STREET.

1796.

ADVERTISEMENT.

THE following sheets originally formed a part of a work now in considerable forwardness, as a reply to Mr. Malone's critical labors on the subject of the Shakspeare MSS. The body of this work required considerable research, and, so large a portion of time for its completion, as to render some further delay unavoidable in the publication of the whole. But this part of the work having been completed and ready for the public eye, I have yielded to the importunities of my friends, who have suggested to me the necessity at this moment, of laying before the public such further particulars as relate to my conduct therein. It will be observed that I have adverted in the course of the following pages to Mr. Malone: and if the animadversions should be deemed irrelevant, I trust, that no other apology is necessary, than the intimation already given, of my having intended this Vindication as an introduction to the work alluded to, and therefore that it was a more eligible plan, not to make any deviation from the method, I at first determined upon pursuing.

A recent circumstance, with which the Public is well acquainted, seems to call for this Vindication, and
even

even (painful as it is) to impose the measure upon me as a solemn duty, and obligation. I allude to the public statement, made by my Son. The world to which he has appealed, will judge and pronounce upon the truth of the allegations, and the weight of the testimonies, which he has laid before them. I beg to assure the public that the refutation of Mr. Malone's book shall be brought forward with all possible speed; in which, whether the papers imputed to Shakspeare are genuine or not, it will be clearly shewn, that he embarked in this enquiry as utterly destitute of the information of a philologist, and the acumen of a Critic; as it will, by his gross and repeated personalities, be manifested, that his selfish and interested views have made him throughout lose sight of the manners of a Gentleman.

ERRATA.

Page 12, last line but 1, after *my* read *friends*
12, line 10, after *to* add *the*
18, — 11, for *it* read *them*
27, — 13, before *Frank* read *John*
30, — 1, for *enter into* read *make*

A

VINDICATION, &c.

THE moſt unequivocal characteriſtic of an enlightened age, is the licence which is indulged to all, of free communication with the public on doubtful, and controverted ſubjects. There are, indeed, ſome queſtions, in the diſcuſſion of which it will be always difficult to perſuade the world, that mutual toleration is the moſt conducive to the intereſts of truth, and the moſt auxiliary to the operation of human reaſon.

But on topics of merely literary reference, that theſe enmities ſhould at all exiſt, muſt appear ſingular, and even paradoxical. For in literary conteſts there is ſcarcely any appeal to any paſſion.

passion. They can neither provoke the hopes, nor vibrate on the fears of mankind, to any considerable degree. It must, therefore, be a satisfactory reflection to those, who have remarked on the history of the human mind, that the mutual hostility, and bigotry, which once deformed the writings of critics and philologists, is at this moment, with few exceptions, totally extinguished. Posterity, when they read the works of Salmasius, or Bentley, will be perplexed, even in finding motives for a spirit so intolerant, and a zeal so intractable on matters of such light, and trivial import.

There are, however, exceptions to a remark, so honorable to the taste, and liberality of our age. There are still some remnants of that *exploded discipline*, which from the disuse into which it has fallen, must at this time, be highly disgusting to the lovers of English literature. The arrogance of schoolmen without their learning, the rancour of controversy without the wit by which it is embellished, must at the present period,

period, demand the severest, and most exemplary animadversion.

Mr. Malone has acquired, it may be said, some degree of literary reputation. It is that sort of reputation, to which a laborious and patient frame of mind, in all the departments of literature has its peculiar pretensions. But neither Mr. Malone, nor any other labourer of the same description, has any privilege of over leaping the province, to the drudgery of which a limited capacity has destined him, while a patient, and charitable world does not deny him the small pittance of fame, that arises out of it. *Illâ se jactet in aulâ.* Mr. Malone, of all writers, has the slightest pretensions to that majesterial character, he has lately assumed, and by virtue of which he undertakes not only to discuss, but to decide on literary questions, as well as to asperse the moral reputations of those, who differ from him in opinion.

The appeal, which I am now about to make

from the sentence, which this gentleman has passed upon the papers in question, primarily originates from that solicitude to vindicate my own character, which it must be naturally supposed, I cannot but feel on this occasion. Whether the critical reasonings of Mr. Malone are solid, or unfounded, whether he is entitled to any degree of reputation, as a philologist, or critic, by the publication of his enquiry, are questions of which the discussion will be postponed, till my answer appears before the public. At present I am merely claiming the attention of the reader to those topics, which relate to my own personal agency in the transaction.

With regard to the manner in which my own character is attacked, it will unquestionably be expected that I should speak fully and amply. It is true Mr. Malone deals only in insinuations; and insinuations, malevolent and slanderous as they are, may easily be repelled. It is true also, that these insinuations are conveyed in a manner, which neither resembles the overbearing acuteness

ness of Dr. Bentley, nor the subtle poignancy of Bishop Warburton. But insinuations may be troublesome, and even noxious; because the dullest being alive may at length, by reiteration and importunity, in some measure, atone for the bluntness and impotence of the shafts with which he assails you. It may indeed be said that these attacks are of a puny and ineffectual nature, but to remain indifferent to such attacks, is a philosophy which I have never arrogated; and it would look like a sort of affected stoicism, to appear silent and unmoved, amidst such malicious and calumniating aspersions.

Through the whole course of his pamphlet, Mr. Malone speaks of the "Impostor," and the "Imposture." I remember in Mr. Locke, a long chapter on words, and the intellectual associations which belong to them. In a well-known essay on the sublime and beautiful Mr. Locke's doctrine is opposed; and it is contended that words are independent of ideas. The author applied this doctrine only to works of taste, but
particularly

particularly to poetry. But in the subject to which Mr. Malone has extended the theory nothing surely can be more ridiculous than the use of words without ideas; and until any thing of the sublime and beautiful be discovered in the prose of that gentleman, the good sense and taste of the world will condemn the use of words which are utterly destitute of a meaning; especially when they are employed on a subject of reasoning and demonstration. Would not the conduct of that judge be ludicrous as well as indecent, who on a criminal matter, should use the words traitor, murderer, or thief, in his address to the jury, concerning the evidence before them? So in the controversy upon the Shakespeare MSS it would have been better reasoning, as well as more candid hostility, to have proved the imposture before he proclaimed the impostor.

In reply to these charges against me, I shall lay before the public some striking documents, which will constitute a most irrefragable system of of evidence in my favor, and furnish the best refutation of what has been alledged against me. I shall first repeat that which I have told the world already, and then I shall enter into the statements, which corroborate and fortify what I have hitherto asserted.

In the preface to my folio collection of *Shakspeare* MSS I stated all the circumstances relative to them, as minutely as my own knowledge of them and the delicacy of my situation permitted me. I shall now repeat the assertion, with no other addition than my solemn protestation of its truth.

" It may be expected, that something should
" be said by the editor, of the manner in which
" these papers came into his hands. He recei-
" ved them from his Son, Samuel William
" Henry Ireland, a young man, then under
" nineteen years of age, by whom the disco-
" very was accidentally made at the house of a
" gentleman of considerable property."
" Amongst

" Amongst a mass of family papers, the
" contracts between Shakspeare, Lowine and
" Condell, and the lease granted by him and
" Hemynge to Michael Fraser, which was first
" found, were discovered, and soon after the
" deed of gift to William Henry Ireland (de-
" scribed as the friend of Shakspeare, in con-
" sequence of his having saved his life on the
" river Thames, when in extreme danger of
" being drowned) and also the deed of trust to
" John Hemynge were discovered. In pursu-
" ing this search, he was so fortunate as to dis-
" cover some deeds very material to the in-
" terests of this gentleman, and such as esta-
" blished beyond all doubt, his title to a consi-
" derable property. In return for this service,
" added to the consideration, that the young
" man bore the same name, and arms, with
" the person, who saved the life of Shakspeare,
" the gentleman promised him every thing re-
" lative to the subject, that had been or should
" be found either in town or at his country
" house. At this house the principal part of
" the

"the papers, with a great variety of books "containing the MSS notes and three MSS "plays, with part of another were difco-"vered."

"Fortified as he is with the opinion of the "unprejudiced and the intelligent, the editor "will not allow that it can be prefumption in "him to fay, that he has no doubt of the truth "and authenticity of that which he lays before "the public. Of this fact he is as fully fatis-"fied, as he is with the honor that has been "obferved to him upon this fubject. So cir-"cumftanced, he fhould not feel juftified in im-"portuning, or any way requefting a gentle-"man, to whom he is known only by obliga-"gation, to fubject himfelf to the impertinence "and licentioufnefs of literary curiofity and ca-"vil, unlefs he fhould himfelf voluntarily come "forward. But this is not all. It was not till "after the mafs of papers received, became vo-"luminous, that Mr. Ireland had any idea of
"printing

" printing them: he then applied for his per-
" miſſion ſo to do,* and this was not obtained,
" but under the ſtrongeſt injunction that his
" name ſhould not appear. This injunction
" has thro' all the ſtages of this buſineſs been
" uniformly declared: and, as this gentleman
" has dealt moſt liberally with the editor, he
" can confidently ſay, that in his turn he has
" with equal openneſs and candour conducted
" himſelf towards the public, to whom imme-
" diately upon every communication made,
" every thing has been ſubmitted without
" reſerve."

The information, which induced me to lay this ſtatement before the public, was derived from written declarations of my ſon, and from

* The reader is here requeſted to underſtand, that the application made to the ſuppoſed original poſſeſſor, was not perſonal, but by letters given by him to his ſon, to be conveyed by him, and by anſwers received, thro' the ſame channel.

those of his friend Mr. Talbot, of the Dublin Theatre. I now present to the world the account of the discovery, as it was written by my son, and which is at this time, in my possession.

"*November* 10th, 1795.

"I was at chambers, when Talbot called
"in, and shewed me a deed, signed Shakspeare.
"I was much astonished, and mentioned the
"pleasure my father would receive, could he
"but see it. Talbot then said, I might shew
"it. I did not for two days: and at the end
"of that term he gave it me. I then pressed
"hard to know, where it was found. After
"two or three days had elapsed, he introduced
"me to the party. He was with me in the
"room, but took little trouble in searching.
"I found a second deed, and a thi d, and two
"or three loose papers. We also discovered
"a deed, which ascertained to the party landed
"property, of which he had then no knowledge.
"In consequence of having found this, he told
"us,

" us, we might keep every deed, every scrap
" of paper relative to Shakspeare. Little was
" discovered in town, but what was above men-
" tioned, but the rest came from the country;
" owing to the papers having been removed from
" London, many years ago.

" S. W. H. Ireland."

Being naturally desirous of obtaining the evidence of Mr. Talbot, to confirm what had been advanced by my son, I applied to the former, and received from him an answer, from which I have made the following extracts.

Carmarthen, November 25, 1795.
" Dear Sir,

"   The gentleman, in whose possession these
" things were found, was a friend of mine; and
" by me your Son Samuel was introduced to his
" acquaintance. One morning in rummaging
" from mere curiosity some old lumber, consist-
" ing of deeds, books, &c. in a closet of my
" friend's house, I discovered a deed with the
" signature

" fignature of William Shakfpeare, which in-
" duced me to read part of it, and on reading
" the words " Stratford on Avon" I was con-
" vinced it was the famous Englifh Bard: with
" permiffion of my friend (whom I will in future
" call Mr. H———) I carried the deed to Sa-
" muel, knowing with what enthufiafm, he and
" yourfelf regarded the works of that author,
" or any trifling article he was poffeffed of;
" though I was prepared to fee my friend Sa-
" muel a little pleafed with what I prefented to
" him, yet I did not expect that great joy he
" felt on the occafion. He told me there was
" nothing known of the hand writing of Shak-
" fpeare, but his fignature to fome deed or will
" in Doctors Commons, and preffed me to carry
" him to H——'s houfe, that he might fee,
" if there was amongft the lumber I had fpoken
" of, any other fuch relique. I immediately
" complied with his requeft. This was Samuel's
" firft introduction. For feveral fucceffive
" mornings we paffed fome hours in examining
" different papers and deeds, moft of which
" were

"were ufelefs, and uninterefting. But our
" labor was rewarded by finding a few more
" relating to Shakfpeare. Thefe we took away,
" but never without H's permiffion. At laft
" we were fo fortunate as to difcover a deed,
" in which our friend was materially concerned.
" Some landed property, which had been long
" the fubject of litigation was here afcertained,
" and H's title to it clearly proved. H. now
" faid in return for this, whatever you and Mr.
" Ireland find among the lumber, be it what it
" may, fhall be your own (meaning thofe things
" which we fhould prize for being Shakfpeare's)
" Mr. H. juft before my departure from Lon-
" don, ftrictly enjoined us never to mention him
" as the poffeffor of the papers. Tho' I wifhed
" until Sam. fhould have completed his re-
" fearches, that little fhould have been faid on
" the fubject, yet I was ignorant, why H. when
" the fearch was finifhed, fhould ftill wifh his
" name concealed. I thought it abfurd and
" could not prevail on him to mention his rea-
" fons; tho' from fome trifling unguarded ex-
" preffion

"preſſion, I was at laſt induced to believe that one of his anceſtors was a cotemporary of Shakſpeare in the dramatic profeſſion; that as he H. was a man ſomewhat known in the world, and in the walk of high life, he did not wiſh ſuch a circumſtance ſhould be made public; this ſuſpicion was, as it will preſently appear, well founded. Whilſt I was in Dublin, I heard to my great joy and aſtoniſhment, that Sam had diſcovered the play of Vortigern and Rowena, the MS of Lear, &c. &c. I was impatient to hear every particular, and principally for that purpoſe made my late viſit to London. I found H. what I always thought him, a Man of ſtrict honor, and willing to abide by the promiſe he made, in conſequence of our finding the deed, by which he benefitted ſo much. I will now explain the reaſon of H's ſecrecy. On account of your deſire to give the world ſome explanation of the buſineſs, and your telling me, that ſuch explanation was neceſſary, I renewed my entreaties to him, to ſuffer us to diſcover

" cover his name, place of abode, and every
" circumſtance of the diſcovery of the papers,
" but in vain. I proceeded to prove as well
" as I could the folly of its concealment, when
" he produced a deed of gift, which he himſelf
" had juſt found in the cloſet, juſt before my
" departure from London, in January laſt, but
" which I had never ſeen before. By this deed
" William Shakſpeare aſſigned to John ———
" who it ſeems was really an anceſtor of our friend
" H. every article contained in an upper room.
" The articles were, furniture, cups, a miniature
" picture, and many other things; but except-
" ing the miniature (which was lately found
" and which was a likeneſs of Shakſpeare him-
" ſelf), and the papers, very few of them re-
" main in H's hands, and the reſt very unfor-
" tunately cannot be traced. It is ſuppoſed too,
" that many valuable papers have been loſt, and
" are deſtroyed, as the whole lumber is never
" remembered to have been at all valued or
" guarded from the hands of the loweſt domeſ-
" tics. When I parted from you a few weeks

ſince

" fince, H. promifed me that the deed of
" gift above mentioned fhould be fent you,
" firft erafing and cutting out the name of the
" grantee.* I hope, my dear Sir, I have omit-
" ted nothing in relating thefe circumftances,
" and though this account may not enable you
" perfectly to fatisfy many, who from an idle
" curiofity would know more, yet the liberal-
" minded, I am fure will allow that you have
" juft reafons for with-holding what is, and is to
" be concealed. I moft earneftly beg you will
" fend me a copy of Vortigern and Rowena, as
" foon as it can conveniently be written, with the
" margin marked, according to the curtailment
" for Stage reprefentation.

"M. Talbot.

" S. Ireland, Efq."

* Within a few days after the receipt of the above, the deed of truft alluded to, was brought to me by my Son, without any erafure, as mentioned in the above letter, and was the deed of truft to John Hemynge, inferted in the folio volume of the Shakfpeare papers.

Upon this authority and with this degree of testimony, I proceeded to the publication of the papers. Yet it may by some be objected, that the weight of the whole evidence collectively taken, is still weak and imperfect, on account of the concealment of the name of the gentleman alluded to. But what inference does this objection authorise? It was such as entirely to militate against any suspicion of fraud in my breast. For had the papers been forged, I could not imagine that the fabricators of it would have left that part of its evidence, to which by ordinary minds, and according to ordinary rules of judgment, the greatest weight is usually attributed, so palpably mutilated, and defective. I could not imagine that it could have been the work of one impostor, when I considered the infinite variety of the papers, and the length of time which must have been consumed on so elaborate a fiction. For it must have been very extraordinary, that of all those who were concerned in the imposture, not one should have
suggested

suggested the necessity of forging completer testimonies, respecting the place, and person, in whose possession they were found.

Besides these reasons, coming as they did through the channel of my Son, I could not suspect their authenticity; and every thing I had remarked of Mr. Talbot during my acquaintance with him, placed him in my judgment beyond even the possibility of suspicion, his fairness and honesty in the transaction appeared invariable. A father is not very eager to entertain surmises, that affect the moral credit of one so dearly connected with him as his only son, and when the same declarations were made by him in the most solemn and awful manner, before crouds of the most eminent characters, who came to my house, I could not suffer myself to cherish the slightest suspicion of his veracity.

The testimonies here adduced it were difficult to resist. But these were not all by which my conduct was governed in this transaction.

I invited to my houfe all who wifhed to gratify their curiofity, by an infpection of the papers. Of thefe, the greater part confifting of the moft celebrated literary characters this age has produced, expreffed their opinions, not in the phrafe of mere affent, but in the unequivocal language of a full and overflowing conviction. Some were even defirous of fubfcribing without folicitation, their names to a certificate, in which their belief might be formally and permanently recorded. The firft of this refpectable lift was the rev. Dr. Parr. I informed this gentleman, that the late James Bofwell, Efq. had requefted my permiffion to annex his name to a certificate, vouching for the validity of the papers and which he drew up for that purpofe. When I fhewed the Doctor, at his requeft what Mr. Bofwell had written the day before, he exclaimed with his characteriftic energy and manner, that it was too feebly expreffed for the importance of the fubject; and begged that he might himfelf dictate to me the following form of a certificate, to which he immediately fubfcribed his own name;

and

and which afterwards received the signatures of the other respectable characters, that are annexed to it.

"We whose names are hereunto subscribed
"have, in the presence and by the favor of
"Mr. Ireland, inspected the Shakspeare papers,
"and are convinced of their authenticity."

 Samuel Parr.
 John Tweddell.
 Thomas Burgess.
 John Byng.
 James Bindley.
 Herbert Croft.
 Somerset.
 If. Heard, Garter King of Arms.
 F. Webb.
 R. Valpy.
 James Boswell.*

* Mr. Boswell, previous to signing his name, fell upon his knees, and in a tone of enthusiasm, and exultation, thanked God, that he had lived to witness this discovery, and exclaimed that he could now die in peace.

        Lauderdale.

Lauderdale.

Rev. J. Scott.

Kinnaird.

John Pinkerton.

Thomas Hunt.

Henry James Pye.

Rev. N. Thornbury.

Jon. Hewlett, Tranſlator of old Records, Common Pleas Office, Temple.

Mat. Wyatt.

John Frank Newton.

The following is a catalogue of the papers above alluded to, dated

February 25th, 1795.

1. Viz. Shakſpeare's profeſſion of faith on two ſmall ſheets of paper.

2. His copy of a letter to Lord Southampton, and Lord Southampton's anſwer.

3. His letter to Richard Cowley, incloſing a curious drawing in pen and ink of himſelf.

4. His

(23)

4. His letter to Anna Hatherwaye, the lady whom he afterwards married, inclofing a braided lock of his hair.

5. Five poetical ftanzas, addreffed to the fame lady, in his own hand writing.

6. His note of hand, payable one month after date to John Hemynge, for five pounds, and five fhillings, together with John Hemynge's receipt the day it became due.

7. A leafe of fix acres of land, and two houfes abutting on the Globe Theatre, granted by William Shakfpeare to Michael Frafer, and figned and fealed by the refpective parties.

8. Deed of agreement between William Shakfpeare and Henry Condell for the weekly payment of a certain fum therein fpecified for the theatrical fervices of the faid Henry Condell, figned and fealed by the refpective parties.

9. Deed

(24)

9. Deed of agreement between William Shakfpeare and John Lowine for the weekly payment of a certain fum therein fpecified for the theatrical fervices of the faid John Lowine, figned and fealed by the refpective parties.

10. A fmall whole length of a tinted drawing, fuppofed to be of Shakfpeare in the character of Baffanio, and on the reverfe fide the whole length of a perfon in the character of Shylock, in its original black frame.

11. An original letter of Queen Elizabeth to Shakfpeare, authenticated by himfelf.

In *March* 1796, In confequence of Mr. Albany Wallis having recently made a difcovery of fome deeds relative to Shakefpeare and Ireland, the following Certificate was figned by the gentlemen, whofe names are annexed to it, after having carefully perufed and collated the faid deeds with thofe in my poffeffion.

" *London,*

" *London, March,* 1796.

" We the underſigned, having inſpected the following deeds in the poſſeſſion of Albany Wallis, Eſq. of Norfolk Street, viz.

" A conveyance, dated 10th *March,* 1612, ſaid to be from Henry Walker to William Shakſpeare, William Johnſon, John Jackſon, and John Hemynges, of a houſe in Black-friars, then or late being in the occupation of one William Ireland; ſigned Wm. Shakſpeare, Jo. Jackſon, and Wm. Johnſon.

" And a deed dated 10th *February,* 1617, being a conveyance ſigned Jo. Jackſon, Wm. Johnſon, and John Hemynges of the ſame premiſes;

" Having alſo inſpected the following papers of Mr. Samuel Ireland of Norfolk Street, viz.

" A MS.

"A MS. Play of Lear, a fragment of
"Hamlet, a play of Vortigern—several deeds,
"witnessed Wm. Shakspeare—several receipts
"and notes of disbursements of monies on ac-
"count of the Globe and certain Theatres—
"familiar letters signed Wm. Shakspeare, and
"other miscellaneous MSS.

"And having compared the hand writing of
"the above papers in Mr. Ireland's possession,
"with the signatures of Shakspeare and He-
"mynge to the deed in Mr. Wallis's hands, as
"well as with the published Fac-similes of the
"autographs of Shakspeare to his last will and
"testament, and to a deed dated 11 *March*, 10
"Jac. I. which came to the hands of Mr. Wal-
"lis, about the year 1760, among the title deeds
"of the Rev. Mr. Fetherstonehaugh, and from
"the character and manner thereof, we declare
"our firm belief in the authenticity of the auto-
"graphs of Shakspeare, and Hemynge, in the
"hands of Mr. Ireland.

Isaac

Isaac Heard, Gr. K. at Arms.
Francis Webb.
Albany Wallis.
Richard Troward.
Jon. Hewlett, Tranflator of old Records, Common Pleas Office, Temple.
John Byng.
Francis Townfend, Windfor Herald.
Gilbert Franklin, Wimpole Street.
Matthew Wyatt, New Inn.
Richard Valpy, Reading.
Jofeph Skinner.
Frank Newton, Wimpole Street.

It may perhaps be almoft unneceffary to ftate that I might have obtained innumerable fignatures to each of the certificates, I have laid before the public, had I reforted to any folicitations for the purpofe. The very refpectable lift of fubfcribers to the publication of Shakfpeare's MSS may be adverted to, as a corroborating proof in favor of their validity and in juftification of my fending them into the world.

I fhall

I shall now present to the reader a voluntary deposition formally drawn on stamped paper, and intended to be taken before a magistrate by my son.

" Samuel William Henry Ireland, of Nor-
" folk Street, in the parish of St. Clement
" Danes, in the county of Middlesex, Gent.
" maketh voluntary oath that since the 16th day
" of Dec. 1794, he this deponent hath at various
" times deposited in the house of this deponent's
" Father, Samuel Ireland, of Norfolk Street
" aforesaid, several deeds and MSS papers
" signed and supposed to be written by Wm.
" Shakspear and others. And this deponent
" farther maketh oath and faith that the deeds
" and MSS papers now open for inspection,
" at his this deponent's father's house, are the
" same which he this deponent so deposited as
" aforesaid; and whereas several disputes have
" arisen concerning the originality of the deeds
" and MS papers aforesaid, and whereas Ed-
" mond Malone, of Queen Anne Street East, of
" the

"the parish of St. Mary-le-Bone, in the said
"county of Middlesex, hath publickly adver-
"vertised or caused to be advertised an assertion
"to the effect that he, the said Edmond Ma-
"lone, had discovered the above mentioned
"papers and MS deeds to be a forgery, which
"assertion may tend to injure the reputation of
"his the said deponent's father. Now this de-
"ponent farther maketh oath that he this de-
"ponent's father, the said Samuel Ireland, hath
"not, nor hath any one of the said Samuel Ire-
"land's family, other than save and except this
"deponent, any knowledge of the manner in
"which he the said deponent, became possessed
"of the said deeds or MSS papers aforesaid or
"any part thereof, or of any circumstance, or
"circumstances relating thereto.

"S. W. H. Ireland.

"Sworn before me this   day of March,
"1796."

Copied verbatim from the hand writing of my Son.

It being thought unneceſſary to enter into a formal depoſition upon the ſubject, my ſon was not ſworn to what he has here depoſed. But Mr. Albany Wallis in May following drew up the advertiſement which I have here ſubjoined, conceiving it more adequate to the purpoſe, which was inſerted in the True Briton, Morning Herald, and other papers.

" Shakſpeare MSS.

" In juſtice to my father, and to remove
" the reproach, under which he has innocently
" fallen, reſpecting the papers publiſhed by him
" as the MSS of Shakſpeare, I do hereby
" ſolemnly declare that they were given to him
" by me, as the genuine productions of Shakſ-
" peare, and that he was and is at this moment
" totally unacquainted with the ſource from
" whence they came, or with any circumſtance
" concerning them, ſave what he was told by
" myſelf, and which he has declared in the
" preface to his publication. With this firm
" belief

" belief and conviction of their authenticity,
" founded on the credit he gave to me and my
" assurances, they were laid before the world.
" This will be further confirmed, when at some
" future period it may be judged expedient to
" disclose the means by which they were ob-
" tained.

" S. W. H. Ireland, Jun."

Witness,
Albany Wallis.
Thomas Trowsdale, Clerk to Messrs.
Wallis and Troward.

Norfolk Street, May 24, 1796.

This is surely very ample testimony, which my son has adduced, to establish my innocence of the imputed forgery. I corroborate this testimony by some further quotations from several letters, written by Mr. M. Talbot, already mentioned to myself and my family, of which the originals are preserved in my possession.

Dublin,

Dublin, 15th *April,* 1796.

"So much do I lament the unfortunate predicament in which Mr. Ireland is involved, that I must do every thing in my power to extricate him from it, consistent with my own honour, and oath. The offer I shall make, therefore will, I hope, be accepted definitively without urging any more proposals, since any others must of necessity be declined by me, though my life were the forfeit for being secret. I will make an affidavit jointly with Sam. " *That Mr. Ireland is innocent of any forgery imputed to him; that he is equally as unacquainted with the discovery of the papers, as the world in general; that he has been only the publisher of them: aud that the secret is known to no more than Sam. myself, and a third person, whom Mr. Ireland is not acquainted with.*"

"If our making this affidavit and the pub-
"lication of it will ferve Mr. Ireland, Sam
"and myfelf are both ready to ftand forward."

"If I may venture an opinion, I ftill think
"it probable that the papers are genuine, that
"Vortigern may have been one of Shakfpeare's
"firft effays at dramatic writing."

"The play of Henry 2d I never have feen,
"nor the manufcript of Vortigern, nor any
"thing relative to it, till I was in London, long
"after the latter was in Mr. Sheridan's hands.
"I muft therefore depend on the veracity of
"others, as to their coming from the fame
"fource as the few manufcripts I faw before I
"left London the firft time."

"Mr. Ireland has defired my opinion re-
"fpecting a plan he propofes of making two
"gentlemen of refpectability acquainted with
"every circumftance, who are to vouch to the
"world for the authenticity of the MSS.
"This

" This will not be confiftent with our promife
" and oath."

" M. Talbot."

It is worth remarking, that about a week before the receipt of this letter (and ftrange as it may appear, at the particular requeft of my fon) a committee confifting of twenty-four refpectable gentlemen met at my houfe, for the purpofe of taking into confideration every circumftance relative to the MSS and the obloquy under which I laboured, in confequence of their publication. This committee met at three different times within the month of April, and my fon was prefent at each of their meetings; at which he propofed that two refpectable perfons who were not members of the committee, fhould be appointed to receive the following information.

" The gentlemen are to be informed
" whence the papers came, the name of the
" gentleman, to whom they belonged, by whom
' difcovered,

" difcovered, and in what place, and manner.
" The fchedule of thofe that remain behind is
" in my father's poffeffion, which he may fhew,
" and which fhall be accounted for by me."

" S. W. H. Ireland."

Copied verbatim from the above paper in his own hand writing, and in his prefence read to the Committee.

It muft be obvious that this propofal does not concur with Mr. Talbot's opinion, as quoted from his letter above.

The following fchedule, likewife, was prefented to the committee by my fon, accompanied with a folemn proteftation, that every article marked with * he had feen, and would in a fhort time be put into my hands: that thofe, which
had

had not this mark, he had only heard were in exiftence, but that he had not feen them.*

* Play of Richard II. in Shakfpeare's MS.
* Play of Henry II.
* ---- of Henry V.
* 62 leaves of K. John.
* 49 leaves of Othello.
* 37 leaves of Richard III.
* 37 leaves of Timon of Athens.
* 14 leaves of Henry IV.
* 7 leaves of Julius Cæfar.
* Catalogue of his books in his own MS.
* Deed by which he became partner of the Curtain Theatre, with Benjamin Kele, and John Hemynges.
* Two drawings of the Globe Theatre on parchment.
* Verfes to Q. Elizabeth.

* This fchedule was voluntarily written by my fon, on the 10th Jan. 1796, in the prefence of Geo. Chalmers, and J. Reeves, Efqrs.

* Verfes

* Verses to Sir Francis Drake.
* Do. to Sir Walter Raleigh.
* Miniature of Shakspeare set in silver.
Chaucer with his MS notes
Book relative to Q. Elizabeth do.
Euphues with do.
Bible with do.
Bochas's Works with his MS notes.
Barclay's Ship of Fools do.
Hollinshed's Chronicle do.
Brief account of his life in his own hand.
Whole length portrait, said to be of him in oil.

The committees alluded to, met three times without arriving at any satisfactory determinations; and as we found it difficult to select two persons to receive the information, my son had promised, Mr. Albany Wallis, as a professional man, voluntarily offered to be himself the depositary of the secret. This trust, as he says, he was induced to accept, in order to clear up any doubt in the mind of the supposed Gentleman as to

any

any part of his property that might be endangered by such disclosure. In consequence of this, my son had frequent interviews with Mr. Wallis. But what was communicated, at those conferences, I have not learned from that gentleman, notwithstanding my reiterated importunities, and most anxious solicitations for that purpose. His uniform answer to these solicitations was, " Do not ask me any questions. It is not pro-" per that you should know the secret. Keep " your mind easy; all will be well in time."

In support of these testimonies, by which my innocence must be clearly established in the judgments of all, who have the slightest pretensions to candor, or sound sense, I will make another quotation from a letter I received from Mr. Talbot, dated Cork, Sept. 16th, 1796.

" Dear Sir,

" Your last letter to me should have been " answered sooner, and the promised affidavit
" been

" been sent, if I could have obtained an answer from your Son to something I wrote about some time since. For without his consenting, if not joining in such a proceeding, I did not think myself authorised, in taking any step whatever."

" I will do all I can to extricate you from any difficulties you may labour under, and not having heard any thing from your son, I will make an affidavit solely, That from my intimacy with him, and my own knowledge of the mystery of the MSS you were innocent of any design to mislead or deceive the public."

" I beg leave to assure you, that I shall feel the greatest pleasure in standing forward to screen you, who are an innocent sufferer."

" M. Talbot."

I have now exhibited to the world all the testimonies of which I am in possession, relative

to

to the discovery of these papers. Whatever impression they are likely to produce, with regard to their authenticity, or spuriousness, they who can doubt my innocence in the transactions, after this statement must be hardened with an incurable malice, or an impenetrable incredulity. Yet for nearly two years, I have been exposed to the animadversions of every half-formed, and puny critic, who has been so far initiated in the elements of language, as to compose a malicious paragraph, and imbibed so much of the spirit of his fraternity, as to mistake petulance and slander for reason and investigation.

Besides these evils, I have reason to complain of the low tricks, and artifices, that have been resorted to, in order to excite the public prejudice against the MSS. I allude to the steps that were taken to preclude the Play of Vortigern from an equitable, and candid hearing. In support of this assertion, let me refer the reader to the following advertisement, published lifhed by Mr. Malone, nearly three months before his enquiry made its appearance.

" Spurious Shakfpeare MSS.

" Mr. Malone's detection of this forgery
" has been unavoidably delayed by the engrav-
" ings having taken more time than was ex-
" pected; but it is hoped that it will be ready
" by the end of this month.
" *Feb.* 16, 1796."

With regard to the delay, which the author of the advertifement feems to lament, I am compelled from my own knowledge of engraving, to conclude that it was wholly intentional. I know, and I fpeak with confidence on the fubject, that with very little diligence the engravings, which Mr. Malone has incorrectly copied from my publication, would require a very fmall portion of time, for their completion. On the 25th of March, however, the play having been already advertifed for the 2d of April, we find the critic, and his fellow labourers the engravers in fuch a ftate of forwardnefs that the
publication

publication was advertised for Thursday March 31st, only two days before the intended representation of the piece. That it might be absolutely impossible that the mischief should not take effect, in several papers of the 1st of April, particularly the Oracle, and Morning Herald, two different and elaborate critiques in praise of Mr. Malone's enquiry made their appearance.

No man can entertain a doubt concerning the purposes, this well constructed delay was meant to answer. The play was ready for re-presentation. It was to make its appeal to the general judgment; and to stand or fall by its decision. But it was the scheme of this critic, to intercept this appeal; to choak, and obstruct the avenues to the public understanding, and to overwhelm it with a torrent of ill-founded prejudices, and anticipated convictions.

I cannot pass over this part of the subject, without remarking, that in order to counteract as much as possible, the mischief of these artifices,

fices, I inserted three days afterwards an advertisement in the papers, in which I animadverted in very severe terms on the temerity of characterising his work, as a detection. In reply to this, Mr. Malone inserts a letter in the Gentleman's Magazine, in which he vindicates himself from the charge, in the following words.

" With respect to the literary temerity ascribed
" to him (Mr. Malone) in characterising his
" work as a detection, he has no apprehension,
" that he shall incur any censure from the judi-
" cious part of mankind, since in this point of
" view he only benches by the side of his learned
" friend the present very respectable Lord Bi-
" shop of Salisbury, who 46 years ago published
" a deservedly admired tract, on a similar sub-
" ject, thus intitled, Milton no Plagiary, or a
" Detection of the forgeries contained in Lau-
" der's Essay, on the imitation of the moderns
" in the Paradise Lost by Milton. By the rev.
" John Douglas, &c."

I have made this quotation, that the world may

may remark the indecent effrontery of drawing an analogy between the rev. Bishop, and the author of the enquiry. Not to mention the wide and unmeasurable distance, between the literary endowments of the two writers, it must be palpable to every one, that there is no resemblance at all between the circumstances of Lauder's forgery, and the discovery of the MSS in my possession.

It is now time for me to close this part of the subject. I have shewn that the manner in which the artifices, of which I complain, have been conducted, is of so mean and pusillanimous a nature, that the malice has been of so low and so contemptible a species, as to reflect very serious dishonour on him, who has condescended to make use of it, because it may naturally be imagined, that a person calling himself a scholar and a gentleman, might have had recourse to worthier and more dignified weapons of controversy.

The other part of this work will be allotted to

to an inveſtigation of the critical attacks, that have been directed againſt the papers, in which I truſt that Mr. Malone will be completely refuted. Perhaps it might be expected of me, that I ſhould advert to the other antagoniſts, who have appeared in the field of the controverſy. Of the firſt of theſe publications, entitled " A Letter to George Steevens, Eſq. con-" taining a Critical examination, &c. &c." As it has been abundantly refuted in a very able pamphlet, entitled " A Comparative Review of " the opinion, &c. &c." I ſhall ſay nothing further. One Waldron likewiſe, has waded into the controverſy, a bad actor and a worſe critic. Theſe are men, on whom I ſhall not animadvert. They who miſtake their vanity for their capacity, and ſuppoſe that they are qualified to perform what they have preſumption to attempt, are a tribe, on whom admonition will be waſted, and rebuke will be ſuperfluous.

But I have confined my reaſoning to Mr. Malone; becauſe, as he is known to the world

by

by what may be emphatically called his literary *labours* on other occasions, so has he distinguished himself by the bulk of his criticisms on this. What Dr. Warburton said of poor Theobald, he would have said with infinitely more justice of this critic: " That what he read he could " transcribe; but as what he thought, if " ever he did think, he could but ill express, " so he read on; and by that means got a cha-" racter of learning, without risquing the im-" putation of wanting a better talent." In the part, however, which he has taken in this controversy, he has brought the only literary quality he has, that of patient, and laborious research, into suspicion. Whether it be the instinctive property of dulness to be dark, and bewildered, in proportion to the efforts it makes to be bright and perspicuous, or that though he has much reading, he has not enough for the office he has arrogated, it is certain that his book abounds with so many blunders, and overflows with so much presumption, that it seems a sort of mixed animal, engendered between

tween a perfevering dulnefs on one fide, and an envious mind on the other.

If I fucceed in proving what I have afferted, I fhall do a very effential fervice to literature itfelf. I fhall have ridded the literary world of a fort of ufurper. I fhall have pulled from his dictatorfhip a man, who has afpired with the moft prefumptuous arrogance to a kind of oracular dignity on thefe matters. I fhall have refcued the underftandings of the public from the dominion of a critic, who, relying on the bulk of his labours, and the ponderous mafs of his refearches, has attempted to give laws on all topics of literature and criticifm.

But fhould I not effect this purpofe, I fhall at leaft retire from the public tribunal with the foothing confcioufnefs, of having vindicated my own character. For I truft I have laid before the world, a mafs of documents, which will effectually lift me above the ftroke of the venomous afperfions that have been directed fo perfeveringly againft me. Should the language I

have

have occafionally ufed in thefe attacks, appear harfh and irritable, I beg to obferve in my juftification, that Mr. Malone's ftrictures are uniformly clothed in the language of afperity and perfonal farcafm; and furely fome indulgence ought to be allowed me, if I repel his attacks with the fame weapons, and reply to unjuft infinuations in the diction of indignant and wounded feelings. It was for the purpofe principally of vindicating myfelf that I have ventured to make this appeal to the public. I might indeed complain of other misfortunes. I might advert to the pecuniary loffes and the confumption of time, which thefe tranfactions have led me into. But when the moft valuable of all human benefits, a clear and unfullied character is endangered, I could not but look on every other evil, as of trivial and fubordinate confideration.

Norfolk Street,
November, 1796.

FINIS.

PUBLISHER'S ADVERTISEMENT

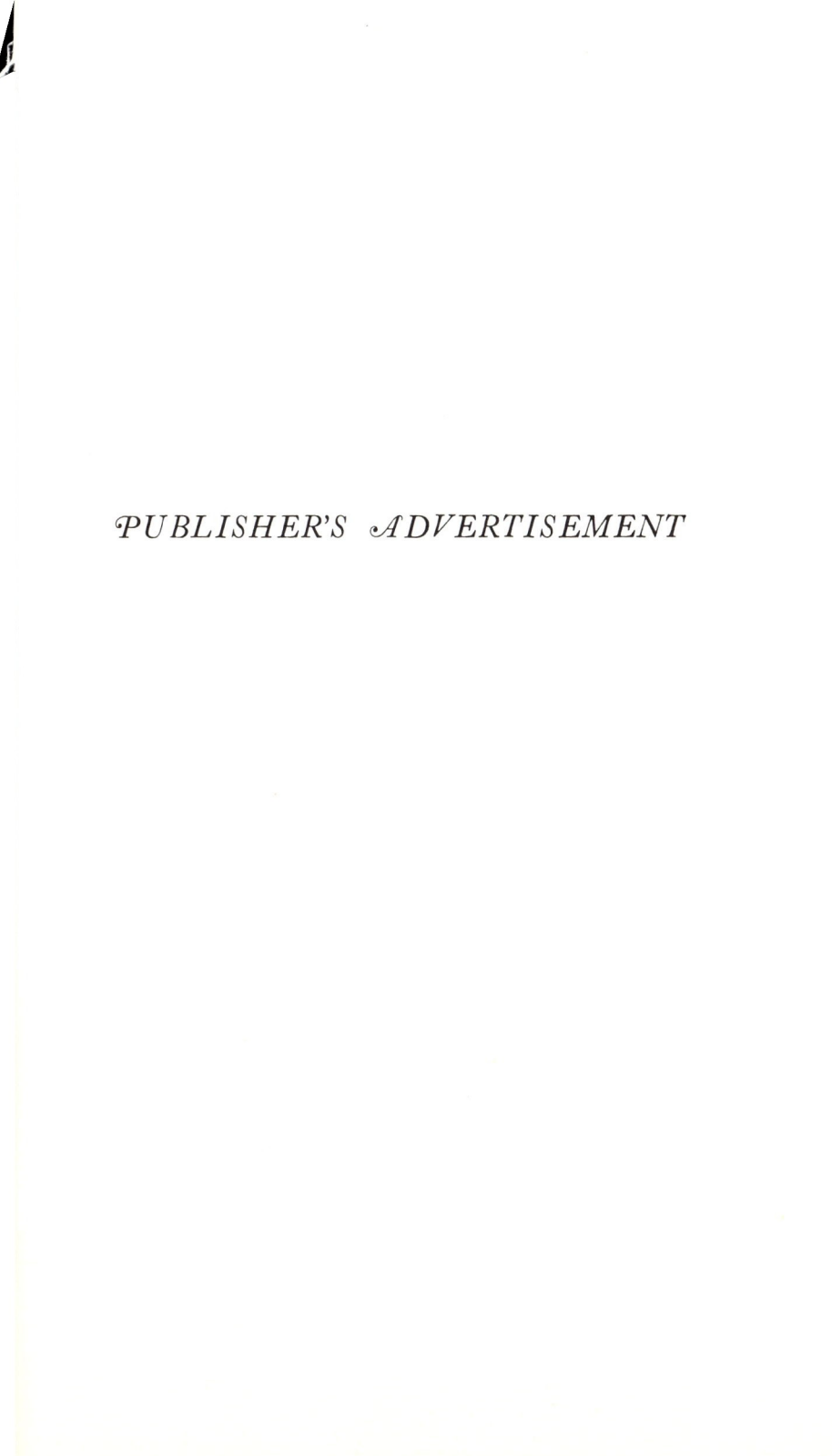

EIGHTEENTH CENTURY SHAKESPEARE

During the one hundred and seven years covered by this series, the reputation of William Shakespeare as poet and dramatist rose from a controversial and highly qualified acceptance by post-Restoration critics and "improvers" to the almost idolatrous admiration of the early Romantics and their immediate precursors. Imposing its own standards and interpretations upon Shakespeare, the Eighteenth Century scrutinized his work in various lights. Certain qualities of the plays were isolated and discussed by a parade of learned, cantankerous, and above all self-assured commentators.

Thirty-five of the most important and representative books and pamphlets are here presented in twenty-six volumes; many of the works, through the very fact of their limited circulation have become extremely scarce, and when obtainable, expensive and fragile. The series will be useful not only for the student of Shakespeare's reputation in the period, but for all those interested in eighteenth century taste, taste-making, scholarship, and theatre. Within the series we may follow the arguments and counter-arguments as they appeared to contemporary playgoers and readers, and the shifting critical emphases characteristic of the whole era.

In an effort to provide responsible texts of these works, strict editorial principles have been established and followed. All relevant editions have been compared, the best selected, and the reasons for the choice given. Furthermore, at least one other copy, frequently three or more, have been collated with the copy actually reproduced, and the collations recorded. In cases where variants or cancels exist, every attempt has been made to provide both earlier and later or indifferently varying texts, as appendices. Each volume is preceded by a short preface discussing the text, the publication history, and, when necessary, critical and biographical considerations not readily available.

1. 1692 **Thomas Rymer**
A Short View of Tragedy (1693)
xvi, 184p.

2. 1693 **John Dennis**
The Impartial Critick: or, some observations upon a late book, entitled, A Short View of Tragedy, written by Mr. Rymer, and dedicated to the Right Honourable Charles Earl of Dorset, etc. (1693)
xvi, 52p.
   1712 **John Dennis**
An Essay on the Genius and Writings of Shakespear: with some Letters of Criticism to the Spectator (1712)
xxii, 68p.

3. 1694 **Charles Gildon [ed.]**
Miscellaneous Letters and Essays, on Several Subjects. Philosophical, Moral, Historical, Critical, Amorous, etc. in Prose and Verse (1694)
xvi, 132p.

4. 1710 **Charles Gildon**
The Life of Mr. Thomas Betterton, the late Eminent Tragedian. Wherein The Action and Utterance of the Stage, Bar, and Pulpit, are distinctly consider'd ... To which is added, The Amorous Widow, or the Wanton Wife ... Written by Mr. Betterton. Now first printed from the Original Copy (1710)
xvi, 176, 87p.

5. 1726 **Lewis Theobald**
Shakespeare restored: or, A Specimen of the Many Errors, As well Committed, as Unamended, by Mr. Pope in his Late Edition of this Poet (1726)
xiii, 194p. 4°

6. 1747 **William Guthrie**
An Essay upon English Tragedy with Remarks upon the Abbe de Blanc's Observations on the English Stage (?1747)
34p.
   1749 **John Holt**
An Attempte to Rescue that Aunciente, English Poet, and

Play-wrighte, Maister Williaume Shakespere, from the Maney Errours, faulsely charged on him, by Certaine New-fangled Wittes and to let him speak for Himself, as right well he wotteth, when Freede from the many Careless Mistakeings, of the Heedless first Imprinters, of his Workes (1749)
94p.

7. 1748 **Thomas Edwards**
The Canons of Criticism and Glossary. Being a Supplement to Mr. Warburton's Edition of Shakespear. Collected from the Notes in that celebrated Work, and proper to be bound up with it. To which are added, The Trial of the Letter *Y* alias Y; and Sonnets (Seventh Edition, with Additions 1765)
368p.

8. 1748 **Peter Whalley**
An Enquiry into the Learning of Shakespeare (1748)
84p.
   1767 **Richard Farmer**
As Essay on the Learning of Shakespeare ... the Second Edition, with Large Additions (1767)
viii, 96p.

9. 1752 **William Dodd**
The Beauties of Shakespeare: Regularly selected from each Play, With a General Index, Digesting them under Proper Heads. Illustrated with Explanatory Notes and Similar Passages from Ancient and Modern Authors (1752)
2v., xxiv, 264; iv, 258p.

10. 1753 **Charlotte Ramsay Lennox**
Shakespear Illustrated ... with Critical Remarks (1753-4)
3v., xiv, 292; iv, 276; iv, 312p.

11. 1765 **William Kenrick**
A Review of Doctor Johnson's New Edition of Shakespeare: In which the Ignorance, or Inattention of That Editor is exposed, and the Poet Defended from the Persecution of his Commentators (1765)
xvi, 136p.
    1766 **Thomas Tyrwhitt**
Observations and Conjectures upon some Passages of

Shakespeare (1766)
ii, 56p.

12. 1769 **Elizabeth Montagu**
An Essay on the Writings and Genius of Shakespear, compared with the Greek and French dramatic Poets. With some remarks upon the misrepresentations of Mons. de Voltaire (1769)
iv, 288p.

13. 1774 **William Richardson**
    1784 Essays on Shakespeare's Dramatic Characters: With an
    1789 Illustration of Shakespeare's Representation of National Character, in that of Fluellen (sixth edition 1812)
xii, 448p.

14. 1775 **Elizabeth Griffith**
The Morality of Shakespeare's Drama Illustrated (1775)
xvi, 528p.

15. 1777 **Maurice Morgann**
An Essay on the Dramatic Character of Sir John Falstaff (1777)
xii, 186p.

16. 1783 **Joseph Ritson**
Remarks Critical and Illustrative of the last Edition of Shakespeare [by George Steevens, 1778], (1783)
viii, 240p.
    1788 **Joseph Ritson**
The Quip Modest; A few Words by way of Supplement to Remarks, Critical and Illustrative on the Text and Notes of the Last Edition of Shakespeare: occasioned by a Republication of that Edition (1788, first issue)
viii, 32p.
With the preface (revised) to the second issue of *The Quip Modest* (1788)
viii p.

17. 1785 **Thomas Whately**
Remarks on some of the Characters of Shakespere, Edited

by Richard Whately (Third edition 1839)
128p.

18. 1785 **John Monck Mason**
    1797 Comments on the Several Editions of Shakespeare's Plays,
    1798 Extended to those of Malone and Steevens (1807)
    xvi, 608p.

19. 1786 **John Philip Kemble**
    Macbeth and King Richard the Third: An Essay, in answer to Remarks on some of the Characters of Shakespeare [by Thomas Whately] (1817)
    xii, 172p.

20. 1792 **Joseph Ritson**
    Cursory Criticisms on the Edition of Shakespeare published by Edmond Malone (1792)
    x, 104p.
    Edmond Malone
    A Letter to the Rev. Richard Farmer, D.D. Master of Emanuel College, Cambridge; Relative to the Edition of Shakespeare, published in 1790. And Some Late Criticisms on that work (1792)
    ii, 40p.

21. 1796 **William Henry Ireland**
    An Authentic Account of the Shakespeare Manuscripts (1796)
    ii, 44p.
    1799 **William Henry Ireland**
    Vortigern, An Historical Tragedy, In five Acts; Represented at the Theatre Royal, Drury Lane. And Henry the Second, An Historical Drama. Supposed to be written by the Author of Vortigern (1799)
    80, iv, 79p.

22. 1796 **Edmond Malone**
    An Inquiry into the Authenticity of Certain Miscellaneous Papers and Legal Instruments, published Dec. 24, 1795. And Attributed to Shakespeare, Queen Elizabeth, and Henry Earl of Southampton (1796)
    vii, 424p.

23. 1796 **Thomas Caldecott**
Mr. Ireland's Vindication of his Conduct, Respecting the Publication of the Supposed Shakespeare Manuscripts (1796)
iv, 48p.

1800 **George Hardinge**
Chalmeriana: or a Collection of Papers ... occasioned by reading a late Apology for the Believers in the Shakespeare papers, by George Chalmers etc. (1800)
viii, 94p.

24. 1798 **Samuel Ireland**
An Investigation of Mr. Malone's Claim to the Character of Scholar, or Critic, Being an Examination of his Inquiry into the Authenticity of the Shakespeare Manuscripts, etc. (1797)
vi, 156p.

25. 1797 **George Chalmers**
An Apology for the Believers in the Shakespeare-Papers which were exhibited in Norfolk Street (1797)
iv, 628p.

26. 1799 **George Chalmers**
A Supplemental Apology for the Believers in the Shakespeare-Papers: Being a Reply to Mr. Malone's Answer, which was early announced, but never published: with a Dedication to George Steevens, and a Postscript (1799)
viii, 656 p.